SHAKESPEARE'S

KING RICHARD THE THIRD.

WITH

INTRODUCTION, AND NOTES EXPLANATORY AND CRITICAL.

FOR USE IN SCHOOLS AND FAMILIES.

BY THE

REV. HENRY N. HUDSON,

PROFESSOR OF SHAKESPEARE IN BOSTON UNIVERSITY.

———•◦•———

BOSTON, U.S.A.:
PUBLISHED BY GINN & COMPANY.
1899.

J. S. CUSHING & CO., PRINTERS, BOSTON.

INTRODUCTION.

History of the Play.

THIS play was preceded by at least two others on the same subject. The first of these was in Latin, written by Dr. Thomas Legge, Master of Caius College, Cambridge, and is said to have been acted at the University as early as 1579. Sir John Harrington, in his *Apology for Poetry*, 1591, speaks of this play as one that "would move Phalaris the tyrant, and terrify all tyrannous-minded men." There is no reason for thinking that Shakespeare ever saw it, or had any knowledge of it. The other was an English drama, printed in 1594, and called "The True Tragedy of Richard the Third : Wherein is shown the death of Edward the Fourth, with the smothering of the two young Princes in the Tower." We have no certain knowledge as to when this piece was written ; though no one doubts that the writing was several years previous to 1594. Shakespeare's drama indicates no acquaintance with it except in two or three slight particulars ; and even here the similarity infers no more knowledge than might well enough have been caught in the hearing. Other resemblances there are indeed, but only such as would naturally result from using a common authority. The older piece has little that can be deemed worthy of notice. The workmanship, though crude and clumsy enough, displays honesty of mind, and is comparatively free from inflation and bombast. The piece is written partly in prose and partly in heavy blank-verse, interspersed with pentameter couplets and rhyming stanzas, and with passages of fourteen-syllable lines. It may be well to add, for the curiosity of the thing, that, after Richard is killed, Report enters, and holds a dialogue with a Page, to give information of divers things not exhibited; after which, two Messengers come in, and unfold what is to be done and who is to reign, all the way from Richard to Queen Elizabeth, the whole winding up with an elaborate panegyric on the latter.

Shakespeare's drama was entered in the Stationers' register on the 20th of October, 1597, and was published the same year, but without the author's name. The play was reprinted in 1598, with "by William Shakespeare" added in the title-page. There was a third issue in 1602, a fourth in 1605, and a fifth in 1613; the last three all claiming to be "newly augmented," though in truth merely reprints of the former two. The play reappeared in the folio of 1623, with many slight alterations of text, with some omissions, and with a few additions, the latter extending in one place to fifty-five consecutive lines. Editors differ a good deal as to the comparative merits of the quarto and folio texts; though all admit that each makes some damaging omissions which the other must be drawn upon to supply. Mr. White leans decidedly to the folio; while Dyce, in his latest edition, prefers the quarto text, on the whole. For myself, I can hardly speak further than that my preference goes sometimes with the one, sometimes with the other. As the additions in the folio do not amount to a general enlargement of the piece, it does not well appear what ground or pretext the quarto of 1602 may have had for claiming to be "newly augmented." Perhaps it was but a publisher's trick, to induce a larger sale of the new edition. The play, however, has very marked diversities of style and workmanship, some parts relishing strongly of the Poet's earlier, others as strongly of his middle period; and I suspect the claim aforesaid may have referred, disingenuously indeed, to changes made in the piece before the issue of 1597.

The great popularity of this play is shown in the number of editions called for, wherein it surpasses any other of the Poet's dramas. For, besides the five quarto issues already mentioned, there were also three others in quarto, after the folio appeared; which proves that there was still a good demand for it in a separate form. It was also honoured beyond any of its fellows by the notice of contemporary writers. It is mentioned by Meres in his *Palladis Tamia*, 1598. Next, we have a very remarkable allusion to it in a poem published in 1614, and entitled *The Ghost of Richard the Third*. The author of the poem gave only his initials, "C. B."; who he was is not positively known; some say Charles Best, others Christopher Brooke: but the strong commendatory verses upon him, which have come down to us from such pens as Ben Jonson, Chapman, and Wither, show him to have been a writer of no little distinction. The Ghost of Richard is made to speak as follows:

> To him that imp'd my fame with Clio's quill,
> Whose magic raised me from Oblivion's den,
> That writ my story on the Muses' hill,
> And with my actions dignified his pen;
> He that from Helicon sends many a rill,
> Whose nectar'd veins are drunk by thirsty men;
> Crown'd be his style with fame, his head with bays,
> And none detract, but gratulate his praise.

Fuller, also, in his *Church History*, and Milton, in one of his political eruptions, refer to the play as well known; and Bishop Corbet, writing in 1617, gives a quaint description of his host at Bosworth, which is highly curious as witnessing both what an impression the play had made on the popular mind, and also how thoroughly the hero's part had become identified with Richard Burbage, the original performer of it :

> Mine host was full of ale and history ;
> And in the morning, when he brought us nigh
> Where the two Roses join'd, you would suppose
> Chaucer ne'er made *The Romaunt of the Rose.*
> Hear him : *See you yon wood? there Richard lay*
> *With his whole army.   Look the other way,*
> *And, lo ! where Richmond in a bed of gorse*
> *Encamp'd himself all night, and all his force :*
> *Upon this hill they met.*   Why, he could tell
> The inch where Richmond stood, where Richard fell.
> Besides what of his knowledge he could say,
> He had authentic notice from the play ;
> Which I might guess by's mustering up the ghosts,
> And policies not incident to hosts ;
> But chiefly by that one perspicuous thing
> Where he mistook a player for a king :
> For, when he would have said, King Richard died,
> And call'd, *A horse, a horse !* he Burbage cried !

Time of the Writing.

As regards the date of the composition, the entry at the Stationers' is the only clear item of external evidence that we have.   The internal evidence makes strongly for as early a date as 1592 or 1593.   The general style, though showing a decided advance on that of the Second and Third Parts of *King Henry the Sixth*, is strictly continuous with it, while the history and characterization of the three plays so knit in together as to make them all of one piece and texture.   And it is all but certain that the Poet's *King Henry the Sixth* was finished as early as 1592.   In Clarence's account of his dream, and in Tyrrel's description of the murder of the young Princes, Shakespeare is out in his plenitude of poetical wealth; and the delineation of Richard is indeed a marvel of sustained vigour and versatile aptness: nevertheless the play, as a whole, evinces somewhat less maturity of power than *King Richard the Second:* in several cases there is great insubordination of the details to the general plan: the points of tragic stress are more frequent, and the dramatic motives more on the surface and more obvious, not to say obtrusive, than may well consist with the reason and law of Art: there is also too much piling-up of curses, or too much ringing of changes in imprecation; and in Richard's wooing of Lady Anne and of Queen Elizabeth there is an excess of dialogical epigram and antiphrastic point, with challenge and retort alternating through a prolonged series of stichometrical speeches: all which shows indeed a prodigious fertility of thought, but betrays withal a sort of mental incontinence, or a want of that self-restraining judgment which, in the Poet's later dramas, tempers all the parts and elements into artistic harmony and proportion. Then too the ethical idea or sense, instead of being duly poised or interfused with the dramatic current, comes too near overriding and displacing it; the pressure of a special purpose marring the organic symmetry of the work.

The close connection between this play and the Third Part of *King Henry the Sixth* is so evident as to leave no occasion for tracing it out in detail. At the opening of the one we have Richard flouting in soliloquy at the "stately triumphs" and "mirthful comic shows" with which, at the close of the other, King Edward had proposed to celebrate the final and full establishment of his cause. It was indeed fitting that, on Richard's first appearance as a dramatic hero, we should overhear him at his old practice of ruminating aloud, and thus familiarizing his thoughts with the villainies which he has it in purpose to enact. Everybody may well be presumed to know how Colley Cibber, being seized with a fit of progress, took upon him to reform Shakespeare's *King Richard the Third* into fitness for the stage. As the original play was too long for representation, his mode of retrenching it to the proper compass was, in part, by transporting into it a scene or two from the foregoing play. I notice the fact, now, merely as showing that he saw the perfect continuity of the two pieces; though, as would seem, he did not perceive the absurdity of thus setting the catastrophe of one at the opening of the other.

Date and Period of the Action.

Historically considered, the play in hand embraces a period of something over fourteen years, namely, from the death of Henry, in May, 1471, to the fall of Richard, in August, 1485. Half of this period, however, is dispatched in the first Act; the funeral of Henry, the marriage of Richard with Lady Anne, and the death of Clarence being represented as occurring all about the same time; whereas in fact they were separated by considerable intervals, the latter not taking place till February, 1478. And there is a similar abridgment, or rather suppression of time between the first Act and the second; as the latter opens with the sickness of King Edward, his seeming reconciliation of the peers, and his death; all which occurred in April, 1483. Thenceforward the events of the drama are mainly disposed in the order of their actual occurrence; the drama being perhaps as true to the history as were practicable or desirable in a work so different in its nature and use.

This drawing together and massing of the scattered events

is eminently judicious; for the plan of the drama required them to be used only as subservient to the hero's character; and it does not appear how the Poet could have ordered them better for developing, in the most forcible manner, his idea of that extraordinary man. So that the selection and grouping of the secondary incidents are regulated by the paramount law of the work; and they are certainly made to tell with masterly effect in furtherance of the author's purpose.

Relation of the Play to History.

As to the moral complexion of Shakespeare's Richard, the incidents whereby his character in this respect transpires are nearly all taken from the historians, with only such heightening as it is the prerogative of poetry to lend, even when most tied to actual events. In the Poet's time, the prevailing ideas of Richard were derived from the history of his life and reign written by Sir Thomas More. More's character as a man is above all suspicion of malice or unfairness or rash judgment; while his clear legal mind and his thorough training in the law rendered him a master in the art of sifting and weighing evidence. His early life was passed in the household of Cardinal Morton, who figures as Bishop of Ely in the play; so that he had ready access to the best sources of information: and this, together with his "monumental probity" and his approved goodness of heart, stamps his work with as much credibility as can well attach to any record of contemporary events. His book was written in 1513, when he was thirty-three years old; and, in speaking of those concerned in the murder of the Princes, he says, "Dighton yet walketh on alive, in good possibility to be hanged ere he die." The character of Richard as drawn by him, and as received in the Poet's time, is well shown in Bacon's *History of Henry the Seventh* :

"The body of Richard, after many indignities and reproaches, the *diriges* and obsequies of the common people towards tyrants, was obscurely buried ; no man thinking any ignominy or contumely unworthy of him that had been the executioner of King Henry the Sixth, that innocent prince, with his own hands ; the contriver of the death of the Duke of Clarence, his brother ; the murderer of his two nephews, one of them his lawful king ; and vehemently suspected to have been the impoisoner of his wife, thereby to make vacant his bed for a marriage within the degrees forbidden. And although he were a prince in military virtue approved, jealous of the honour of the English nation, and likewise a good law-maker, for the ease and solace of the common people ; yet his cruelties and parricides, in the opinion of all men, weighed down his virtues and merits ; and, in the opinion of wise men, even those virtues themselves were conceived to be rather feigned and affected things, to serve his ambition, than true qualities ingenerate in his judgment and nature."

Nevertheless much has since been written to explode the current history of Richard, and to lessen, if not remove, the abhorrence in which his memory had come to be held. The Poet has not been left without his share of criticism and censure for the alleged blackening of his dramatic hero. This attempt at reforming public opinion was led off by Sir George Buck, whose *History of Richard the Third* was published in 1646. The general drift of his book is well indicated by Fuller in his *Church History*, who is himself high authority on the matters in question : "He eveneth Richard's shoulders, smootheth his back, planeth his teeth, and maketh him in all points a comely and beautiful person. Nor stoppeth he here; but, proceeding from his naturals to his morals, maketh him as virtuous as handsome; concealing most, denying some, defending others, of his foulest facts, wherewith in all ages since he standeth charged on record. For mine own part, I confess it is no heresy to maintain a paradox in history; nor am I such an enemy to wit as not to allow it leave harmlessly to disport itself for its own content, and the delight of others. But when men do it cordially, in sober sadness, to pervert people's judgments, and therein go against all received records, I say that singularity is the least fault that can be laid to such men's charges."

Something more than a century later, the work was resumed and carried on with much acuteness by Horace Walpole in his *Historic Doubts*. And several other writers have since put their hands to the same task. Still the old judgment seems likely to stand, the main substance thereof not having been much shaken yet. Dr. Lingard has carried to the subject his usual candour and research; and, after dispatching the strong points urged on the other side, winds up his account of Richard thus: "Writers have indeed in modern times attempted to prove his innocence; but their arguments are rather ingenious than conclusive, and dwindle into groundless conjectures when confronted with the evidence which may be arrayed against them." The killing of the two Princes formed the backbone of the guilt laid at Richard's door. That they did actually disappear, is tolerably certain; that upon him fell whatever advantage could grow from their death, is equally so; and it is for those who deny the cause uniformly assigned at the time, and long after, for their disappearance, to tell us how and by whom they were put out of the way. And Sharon Turner, who may be justly ranked among the severest sifters of historic fictions and fables, is constrained to admit Richard's murder of his nephews ; and, so long as this blood-stain remains, the scouring of others, however it may diminish his crimes, will hardly lighten his criminality.

But even if Shakespeare's delineation were proved to be essentially untrue to Richard as he was in himself, this would not touch the standing of his work as a dramatic reproduction of historical matter. For the Poet's vindication on this score, it suffices that his Richard, so far at least as regards the moral complexion of the man, is substantially the Richard of the chroniclers, and of all the historical authorities received and studied in his time. Besides, to satisfy the nice scruples and queries of historic doubters and dialecticians, is not a poet's business : his concern is with Truth in her operative form, not in her abstract essence ; and to pursue the latter were to anatomize history, instead of representing it. Whether, then, Richard was in fact guilty of such and such crimes, matters little ; it being enough that he was *generally believed to be so,* and that this belief was the mother-principle of those national events whereon the drama turns. That Richard was a prince of abundant head ; that his government was in the main wise and just ; that he was sober in counsel, brave in the field, and far-sighted in both ; — all this only renders it the harder to account for that general desertion which left him almost naked to his foes, but by such a deep and wide-spread conviction of his wickedness as no puttings-forth of intellect could overcome. Thus his fall, so sudden and complete, was mainly in virtue of what he *was thought to be.* And forasmuch as the character generally set upon him at the time, if not the essential truth regarding him, was the stuff out of which were spun his overthrow, and the consequent opening of a new social and political era; such therefore was the only character that would cohere with the circumstances, so as to be capable of dramatic development.

Source of the Historic Matter.

More's history, as it is commonly called, was adopted by both Hall and Holinshed into their *Chronicles*. In that noble composition, the main features of the man are digested and drawn together as follows:

" Richard, the third son, was in wit and courage equal with either of them; little of stature, ill-featured of limbs, crook-backed, his left shoulder much higher than his right, hard-favoured of visage; malicious, wrathful, envious, and from afore his birth ever froward. Free he was called of dispense, and somewhat above his power liberal: with large gifts he gat him unsteadfast friendship, for which he was fain to pill and spoil in other places, and gat him steadfast hatred. He was close and secret, a deep dissembler, lowly of countenance, arrogant of heart; outwardly companionable where he inwardly hated, not letting to kiss whom he thought to kill; despiteous and cruel, not for evil will always, but oftener for ambition, and for the surety or increase of his estate. His face was small, but such, that at the first aspect a man would judge it to savour of malice, fraud, and deceit. When he stood musing, he would bite and chaw his nether lip; as who said that his fierce nature in his cruel body always chafed, stirred, and was ever unquiet: besides that the dagger which he wore he would, when he studied, with his hand pluck up and down in the sheath to the midst, never drawing it fully out." Again the same writer notes him as being inordinately fond of splendid and showy dress; thus evincing an intense craving to be "looked on in the world," and to fascinate the eyes of men.

Shakespeare's Richard, morally speaking, is little else than this descriptive analysis reduced to dramatic life and expression; except, perhaps, that More regards him as a hypocrite by nature, and cruel from policy, whereas the Poet rather makes his cruelty innate, and his hypocrisy a politic art used in furtherance of his ambition.

Growth of Richard's Character.

In the present play, we have the working-out of the hero's character as already formed; the processes of its formation being set forth in the preceding plays of *King Henry the Sixth;* which is sufficient cause for adverting to a few points there delivered. And in this case, as in sundry others, the Poet suggests, at the very outset, the pivot on which the character mainly turns. When we first meet with Richard, Clifford taunts him:

> Hence, heap of wrath, foul indigested lump,
> As crooked in thy manners as thy shape!

And again in the same scene he is called "foul stigmatic"; because the stigma set on his person is both to others the handiest theme of reproach, and also to himself the most annoying; like a huge boil on a man's face, which, for its unsightliness, his enemies see most, and, for its soreness, strike first. And Richard's personal deformity is regarded not only as the proper outshaping and physiognomy of a certain original malignity of soul, but also as aggravating that malignity in turn; his shape having grown ugly because his spirit was bad, and his spirit growing worse because of his ugly shape. For his ill-looks invite reproach, and reproach quickens his malice; and because men hate to look on him, therefore he craves all the more to be looked on; and, for the gaining of his wish in this point, he covets nothing so much as the being able through fear to compel that which inclination denies. Thus experience generates in him a most inordinate lust of power; while the circumstantial impossibility of coming at this save by crime puts him upon such a course of intellectual training and practice as may enable him to commit crimes, and still bar off the natural consequences.

Moreover his extreme vanity results in a morbid sensitiveness to any signs of neglect or scorn; and these being especially offensive to himself, he therefore has the greater delight in venting them on others: as taunts and scoffs are a form of power which he feels most keenly, he thence grows fond of using them as an apt form whereby to make his power felt. For even so bad men naturally covet to be wielding upon others the causes and instruments of their own sufferings. Hence the bitterly-sarcastic humour which Richard indulges so freely, and with such prodigious effect. Of course his sensitiveness is keenest touching the very particular wherein his vanity is most thwarted and wounded: he thinks of nothing so much as the ugliness that balks his desire, and resents nothing so sharply as the opinion or feeling it arrays against him. Accordingly his first and heaviest shots of sarcasm are at those who twit him on that score. So, in the scene where the Lancastrian Prince of Wales is killed, Richard seems unmoved till the Prince hits him in that eye, when his wrath takes fire at once, and bursts out in the reply, "By Heaven, brat, I'll plague you for that word."

All which explains the cause of Richard's being so prone

to "descant on his own deformity." His thoughts brood upon this, because it is the sorest spot in his condition ; and he becomes intent on making it the source of a dearer gratification than any it deprives him of, — the consciousness of such mental powers as can bear him onward and upward in spite of those disadvantages. Thus his sense of personal disgrace begets a most hateful and malignant form of pride, — the pride of intellectual force and mastery. Hence he comes to glory in the matter of his shame, to exaggerate it, and hang over it, as serving to approve, to set off, and magnify his strength and fertility of wit; as who would say, Nature indeed made me the reproach and scorn of men, nevertheless I have made myself their wonder and applause ; and though my body be such that men could not bear the sight of me, yet I have managed to charm their eyes.

In this way the man's galling wakefulness to his own unsightly shape festers and malignifies into a kind of self-pleasing virulence. Nor is this all. For, on much the same principle, he nurses to the highest pitch his consciousness also of moral deformities. So far from palliating his wickedness to himself, or skulking behind any subterfuges, or trying in any way to dodge the sense of it, he rather makes love to it, and exults in spreading it out and turning it round before his inward eye, and even stimulates his vision of it ; as if he were so charmed with the sight that he could not bear to lose any moment of it. To succeed by wrong, to rise by crime, to grow great by inverting the moral order of things, is in his view the highest proof of genius and skill. So he cooks both his moral and personal ugliness into food of intellectual pride. The worse he sees himself to be, the higher he stands in his own esteem, because this argues in him the greater superiority to other men in force of mind.

This aspect of the man is indeed startling, but I think it is fully borne out by his soliloquies in the Third Part of *King Henry the Sixth;* especially that in Act iii., scene 2 :

> Well, say there is no kingdom, then, for Richard ;
> What other pleasure can the world afford ?
> I'll make my heaven in a lady's lap,
> And deck my body in gay ornaments,
> And witch sweet ladies with my words and looks.
> O miserable thought ! and more unlikely
> Than to accomplish twenty golden crowns !
> Why, Love forswore me in my mother's womb :
> And, for I should not deal in her soft laws,
> She did corrupt frail Nature with some bribe,
> To shrink mine arm up like a wither'd shrub ;
> To make an envious mountain on my back,
> Where sits deformity to mock my body ;
> To shape my legs of an unequal size ;
> To disproportion me in every part.
> Then, since this Earth affords no joy to me,
> But to command, to check, to o'erbear such
> As are of better person than myself,
> I'll make my heaven to dream upon the crown,
> And, whiles I live, t' account this world but Hell,
> Until my head, that this mis-shaped trunk bears,
> Be round impalèd with a glorious crown.
> Why, I can smile, and murder whiles I smile ;
> And cry *Content* to that which grieves my heart ;
> And wet my cheeks with artificial tears,
> And frame my face to all occasions :
> I can add colours to the chameleon ;
> Change shapes with Proteus for advantages ;
> And set the murderous Machiavel to school.

So much for the Poet's Richard as his character is seen growing and taking shape. His innate malice has had fitting exercise and nurture amidst the rancours and fierceness of civil slaughter : by his immunities of rank and station, his native strength of will has been pampered into a towering

audacity of thought and purpose : the constant presence and
ever-shifting forms of danger have trained him to a most pro-
tean hypocrisy : he is a consummate master alike in the arts
of dissembling and of simulation ; can counterfeit brusque-
ness, meekness, innocence, humility, sorrow, anger, indignation, artlessness, and piety ; and can play the blusterer, the
wag, the boon companion, the penitent, the lover, the devo-
tee, the hot partisan, the hearty friend, the cool adviser, and
the passionate avenger ; each in turn, or several of them
together, as the occasion prompts, or the end requires.   But,
whatever sentiment he is feigning, or whatever part he is
playing, his biting, malicious wit is ever in action, as if this
were an original impulse with him, and the natural pastime
of his faculties.   Many strong instances of this occur in the
plays where he is growing, but nothing to what we have from
the full-grown Richard in the play that bears his name.
Any quotations in this kind would use up too much space ;
so I must rest with noting that we have a good sample in
Act i., scene 3, where, coming abruptly into the presence of
the Queen and her friends, he counterfeits passion as the
language of grieved and injured virtue ; and a still better
one in Act iv., scene 2, where he plays off his caustic banter
on "the deep-revolving witty Buckingham."   In his pride
of intellectual superiority, he looks with intense scorn on all
in any sort touched with honesty ; they are game to him ;
and his supreme delight is in mocking at such "simple gulls"
as Clarence, Hastings, Stanley, Buckingham ; and it is by his
dry, stinging pungency of speech that he engineers his contempt of them to the spot.   Those whom it is not in his
power or his policy to kill he loves at least to torment with
wounding flouts.

Richard's Intellect.

I have said that the moral complexion of Shakespeare's Richard was mainly taken from the historians. Intellectually, however, his proportions are drawn much beyond what the history accords him. I suppose there was very good reason for this. For, to have set forth such a moral physiognomy in dramatic form, with only his actual endowment of mind, would scare consist with so much of pleasure in his gifts as was required to countervail the horror of his crimes. Such a measure of depravity, stripped of the disguise which it neces-sarily keeps up in real life, might indeed be valuable as truth, but would hardly do as poetry. Which may aptly suggest the different laws of History and Art. Now the method of History is to please because it instructs ; of Art, to instruct because it pleases. Such, at least, is the best way I can find of marking the difference in question. The forms of poetry are relished, not as being fitted to facts, but as they fit the mind. Nor does this infer any defect of real instructiveness in Art ; for whatever pleasure springs in virtue of such cor-respondence with our better nature carries refreshment and invigoration in its touch.

Practically, no man ever understood this thing better than Shakespeare. Nor, perhaps, is his understanding thereof better shown anywhere than in Richard. The lines of his wickedness as traced in history are somewhat deepened in the play, and its features are charged with boisterous life ; making, all together, a fearful picture, and such as, without counterpoising attractions, would be apt to shock and revolt the beholder. But his intellectuality is idealized so far and in such sort as to season the impression of his moral deformity with the largest and most various mental entertainment. If

Richard is all villain, he is an all-accomplished one. And any painful sense of his villainy is spirited away by his thronging diversions of thought, his unflagging gayety of spirits, his prompt, piercing, versatile wit. Nay, his very crimes beget occasion for these enchantments, while every demand seems in effect to replenish his stock : and thus the hateful in his character is so compensated by the admirable, that we are more than reconciled to his company, though nowise reconciled to his crimes.

This point is well illustrated in Richard's wooing of Lady Anne, where the rays of his character are all gathered, as it were, into a focus. Now, whatever may have been the facts in the case, it is certain that Richard was at the time generally believed by the Lancastrians to have had a hand in killing both Henry the Sixth and Edward his son. It is also certain that within two years after their death Richard was married to Edward's widow, who must in all reason be supposed to have shared in the common belief of her party. How that party felt on the subject well appears in that the late King was revered by them as a martyr, and his tomb hallowed as the abode of miraculous efficacies ; for which cause Richard had his bones removed to a more secluded place. On Richard's part, the chief motive to the marriage probably was, that he might have a share in the immense estates of the lady's father, who was Richard Neville, the great Earl of War-wick, known in history as "the King-maker," and in Shake-speare as "the setter-up and puller-down of kings." For, as Clarence, having married the elder daughter, grasped at the whole ; and as Richard proposed by taking the younger to acquire a part ; hence arose the fierce strife between them, from which grew the general persuasion that Richard was somehow the cause of his brother's death. Perhaps, as indicating the manner and spirit of the contest, it should be mentioned that Clarence, to thwart Richard's purpose, at first had the lady concealed from his pursuit several months in the disguise of a cook-maid ; and that, when at last the former saw he could not prevent the marriage, he swore that the latter " should not part the livelihood with him."

So that the Poet is nowise answerable for this difficulty : it was in the history ; and the best he could do was to furnish such a solution of it as would stand with the conditions of dramatic effect. Before solving the difficulty, however, he greatly augments it by suppression of time. Richard begins and finishes his courtship of the lady over the very coffin of the royal saint whose death *she* is mourning, and whom *he* is supposed to have murdered. Yet his triumph, such is the Poet's management, seems owing not so much to any special vice or defect in her as to his witchcraft of tongue and wit, so put in play as to disconcert all her powers of resistance. In a word, it is because the man is simply irresistible. And it should be remembered in her behalf, that his art succeeds equally in beguiling King Edward, Clarence, Hastings, Buckingham, and others. His towering audacity, which, springing from entire confidence in his powers, prevails in part by the very boldness of its attempts ; his flexibility and suppleness of thought, turning himself indifferently to all occasions, forms, and modes of address ; his perfect self-possession and presence of mind, never at a loss for a shift, nor betrayed into a misstep, nor surprised into a pause ; his wily dissimulation, and more wily frankness, silencing her charges by pleading guilty to them, parrying her blows by inviting them, disarming her hatred by owning its justice ; and his simulating deep contrition for past misdeeds, and the inspiration of her virtue and beauty as the cause of it;—such are the parts of the sly, subtle, unfearing, remorseless Richard that are wrought out in his courtship of Lady Anne.

The scene is indeed far from being the best, or even among the best, in the play; but it combines a remarkable variety of characteristic points, and happily exemplifies the Poet's method of diverting off the offensiveness of Richard's acts by the entertainment of his gifts. In these respects, we have a repetition of the scene afterwards, when he in like manner triumphs, or seems to triumph, over the fears and scruples of Elizabeth. But indeed the Poet's work is shaped and ordered from the outset with a special view to the point in hand; the utmost care being taken, that in our first impression of the full-grown Richard his thought-swarming head may have the start of his bloody hand. Which order, by the way, is clean reversed in Cibber's patch-work preparation of the play; the murder of the sainted Henry being there foisted in at the opening, so that admiration of Richard's intellect is forestalled by abhorrence of his wickedness. Assuredly it is neither wise nor right thus to tamper with the Poet's workmanship. In the play as he made it, the opening soliloquy, so startling in its abruptness, and so crammed with poetry and thought, has the effect of duly pre-engaging our minds with the hero's active, fertile, scheming brain: our impression is of one unrelenting indeed, and incapable of fear, but who looks well before he strikes, and who is at least as remarkable for his powers of mind as for his abuse of them. Thus, in the original drama, our feelings are from the first properly set and toned to the scope and measure of the terrible as distinguished from the horrible; the reverse of which takes place in the Cibberian profanation. And the organic law of the work plainly requires that some such initiative be given to the penetrating and imperturbable sagacity which presides over all the other elements of Richard's character, and everywhere pioneers to his purpose.

Richard's irresistible arts of insinuation, how he can at once, and almost in the same breath, plant terrors and sweeten them away, is well shown in the brief scene with Ratcliff and Catesby, when he is preparing to meet the invading Richmond :

> *Rich.* Some light-foot friend post to the Duke of Norfolk : —
> Ratcliff, thyself, — or Catesby ; where is he ?
> *Cate.* Here, my good lord.
> *Rich.* Fly to the Duke. — [*To* RAT.] Post thou to Salisbury :
> When thou comest thither, — [*To* CATE.] Dull, unmindful villain,
> Why stay'st thou here, and go'st not to the Duke ?
> *Cate.* First, mighty liege, tell me your Highness' pleasure,
> What from your Grace I shall deliver to him.
> *Rich.* O, true, good Catesby : bid him levy straight
> The greatest strength and power he can make,
> And meet me suddenly at Salisbury.

Here, by his bland apology implied in "O, true, good Catesby," which drops so easily that it seems to spring fresh from his heart, he instantly charms out the sting of his former words ; and we feel that the man is knit closer to him than ever. Yet his kingly dignity is not a whit impaired, nay, is even heightened, by the act, partly from his graciousness of manner, and partly from his quick art in putting the apology under a sort of transparent disguise.

It should be observed that Richard, with all his inborn malignity, still does not properly hate those whom he kills : they stand between him and his purpose ; and he has "neither pity, love, nor fear," that he should blench or stick to hew them out of the way. His malice wantons in biting taunts and caustic irony ; he revels in teasing and galling

others with bitter mocks and jerks; but he is too self-repres-
sive and too politic to let his malice run out in gratuitous
cruelties.   A reign of terror planted and upheld by a guil-
lotine of malicious wit is as far as his ambition and sagacity
will permit him to go in that direction.   For Shakespeare
could never have conceived of the English people as tolerat-
ing even for a day a reign of terror founded on a guillo-
tine of steel.   And Richard is prudent enough to restrain
his innate virulence from attempting so suicidal a course as
that.   But he has at the same time a certain redundant, im-
pulsive, restless activity of nature, so that he cannot hold
still; and as his thought seizes with amazing quickness and
sureness where and when and how to cut, so he is equally
sudden and sure of hand.   It is as if such an excess of life
and energy had been rammed into his little body as to strain
and bulge it out of shape.

Alleged Faults of the Delineation.

I have observed that Richard is a villain with full consciousness; and that, instead of endeavouring in any way to
hide from his crimes, he rather fondles and caresses them
as food of intellectual pride.   And such is Coleridge's view.
" Pride of intellect," says he, "is the characteristic of Richard carried to the extent of even boasting to his own mind
of his villainy.   Shakespeare here develops, in a tone of sub-
lime morality, the dreadful consequences of placing the moral
in subordination to the mere intellectual being."   In this respect, Richard transcends the Poet's other crime heroes, Iago
and Edmund, who, with all their steeping in hell-venom, are
still unable to look their hellish purposes steadily in the face,
and seek refuge in certain imaginary wrongs which it is the

part of manhood to revenge either on particular persons or on society at large.

This feature of Richard transpires audibly, and with not a little of special emphasis, in his soliloquies, both those in the Third Part of *King Henry the Sixth*, and also those in the present play. It has been questioned, and is indeed fairly questionable, whether the delineation in this point does not overpass the natural limits of human wickedness. One of the authors of *Guesses at Truth* thinks the Poet " has somewhat exaggerated the diabolical element" in the speeches in question. " If," says he, " we compare the way in which Iago's plot is first sown, and springs up, and gradually grows and ripens in his brain, with Richard's downright enunciation of his projected series of crimes from the first, we may discern the contrast between the youth and the mature manhood of the mightiest intellect that ever lived upon Earth." Again, after noting how Richard's sense of personal deformity acts as an irritant of his innate malice, the writer proceeds thus : " I cannot but think that Shakespeare would have made a somewhat different use even of this motive, if he had rewritten the play in the maturity of his intellect. Would not Richard then, like Edmund and Iago, have palliated and excused his crimes to himself, and sophisticated and played tricks with his conscience?" And the writer affirms withal, that "it is as contrary to nature for a man to anatomize his heart and soul thus, as it would be to make him dissect his own body."

Metaphors are rather ticklish things to reason with ; and the sentence last quoted goes somewhat to discredit the writer's criticism in certain points which I am apt to think well taken. For in fact men often do practise a degree of self-anatomy in their mental and moral parts, such as were

obviously impossible as regards their bodily structure. Now
Richard as drawn by the Poet in action no less than in
speech has a dare-devil intellectuality, in the strength of
which, for aught I 'can see, he might inspect and scrutinize
himself as minutely and as boldly as he would another person,
or as another person would him. And why might he not,
from the same cause, grow and harden into a habit of facing
his blackest purposes as unflinchingly as he does his unsightly
person, and even of taking pleasure in over-painting their
wickedness to himself, in order at once to stimulate and to
gratify his lust of the brain? And does not his most dis-
tinctive feature, as compared with Iago and Edmund, stand
mainly in this, that intellectual pride is in a more exclusive
manner the constituent of his character? The critic, be it
observed, specially faults certain of Richard's soliloquies, as
if there were something exceptionally wrong in these ; and
the question with me is, whether these are not in perfect
keeping with his character as transpiring in action throughout the play. For it is manifest that, in what he does, no
less than in what he there says, his hypocrisy is without the
least shade of self-delusion. The most constant, the most
versatile, the most perfect of actors, he is never a whit taken
in by his own acting : he has, in consummation, the art to
conceal his art from others ; and because this is what he
chiefly glories in, therefore he takes care that it may not become in any degree a secret to himself. Moral obliquity so
played as to pass for moral rectitude is to him the test and
measure of intellectual strength and dexterity ; for which
cause he delights not only to practise it, but also to contem-
plate himself while practising it, and even while designing
it. And herein he differs from all real-life actors, where it
is hardly possible but that hypocrisy and self-deceit should

slide into each other: hence it is that hypocrites are so apt to end by turning fanatics, and *vice versa*, as common observation testifies.

But this is making Richard out an improbable character, — a character running to a height of guilt where no man could sustain himself in being? Perhaps so. And my purpose is not so much to vindicate the soliloquies as to suggest whether the charge raised from them will not hold equally against the whole delineation. If I am right in thinking that the soliloquies strictly cohere with his general action, it follows that both are in fault, or neither: so that, if the Poet be there in error, he is at least consistently so. Instead, therefore, of rejecting the forecited criticism, I should rather incline to extend it over the substance and body of the play; in the very conception of which we seem to have somewhat of the mistake, so incident to youthful genius, of seeking for excellence rather by transcending Nature than by closing with her heartily, and going smoothly along with her.

Richard's Abnormal Individuality.

It is plain that such a man as Richard must either cease to be himself, or else must be himself alone. Isolation, virtual or actual, is his vital air, the breath, the necessary condition of his life. One of his character, without his position, would have to *find* solitude; Richard, by his position, has the alternative of creating it: the former must be where none others are; the latter, where all others are in effect as if they were not. For society is in its nature a complexion of mutualities, and every rule pertaining to it works both ways: it is a partnership of individualities, some of them subordinate indeed, and some superior; but yet in such sort as to presuppose a net-work of ties running and recurring from each to each; so that no one can urge a right without inferring a duty, nor claim a bond without owning himself bound. But Richard's individuality can abide no partner, either as equal, or as second, or in any other degree. There is no *sharing* any thing with him, in however unequal portions; no acting *with* him, as original, self-moving agents, but only *from* him, as the objects and passive recipients of his activity. Such is the form and scope of his individuality, that other men's cannot stand in subordination to it, but must either crush it, or fly from it, or be absorbed into it; and the moment any one goes to acting otherwise than as a limb of his person, or an organ of his will, there is a virtual declaration of war between them, and the issue must hang on a trial of strength or of stratagem.

Hence there is, properly speaking, no interaction between Richard and the other persons of the drama. He is the all-in-all of the scene. And herein is this play chiefly distinguished from the others, and certainly, as a work of art, not distinguished for the better, that the entire action, in all its parts and stages, so far at least as it has any human origin and purpose, both springs from the hero as its source, and determines in him as its end. So that the drama is not so much a composition of co-operative characters, mutually developing and developed, as the prolonged yet hurried outcome of a single character, to which the other persons serve but as exponents and conductors; as if he were a volume of electricity disclosing himself by means of others, and quenching their active powers in the very process of doing so. The most considerable exception to this is Queen Margaret, whose individuality shoulders itself in face to face with Richard's; her passionate impulse wrestling evenly with his deliberate purpose, and her ferocious temper being provoked to larger and hotter eruptions by all attempts at restraint or intimidation. This, to be sure, is partly because she can *do* nothing; while at the same time her tongue is all the more eager and powerful to blast, forasmuch as she has no hands to strike.

The preceding remarks may go far to explain the great and lasting popularity of this play on the stage. There being no one to share with the hero in the action and interest of the piece, this renders it all the better for theatrical starring; for which cause most of the great actors have naturally been fond of appearing in it, and play-goers of seeing them in it. Besides, the hero, as before remarked, is himself essentially an actor, though an actor of many parts, sometimes acting one of them after another, and sometimes several of them together: and the fact that his character is much of it assumed, and carried through as a matter of art, probably makes it somewhat easier for another to assume. At all events, the difficulty, one would suppose, must be much less in proportion to the stage-effect than in reproducing the deep tragic passions of Lear and Othello, as these burst up from the original founts of nature.

Workings of his Conscience.

Richard, however, is not all hypocrite: his courage and his self-control at least are genuine; nor is there any thing false or counterfeit in his acting of these. And his strength of will is exerted even more in repressing his own nature than in oppressing others. Here it is, perhaps, that we have the most admirable feature of the delineation. Such a vigour of self-command, the central force of all great characters, seldom fails to captivate the judgment, or to inspire something like respect; and, when carried to such a height as in Richard, it naturally touches common people with wonder and awe, as being wellnigh superhuman. In this respect, he strongly resembles Lady Macbeth, that he does absolute violence to his nature in outwrestling the powers of conscience. In his waking moments, he never betrays, except in one instance, any sense of guilt, any pangs of remorse; insomuch that he seems to have a hole in his head, where the moral faculties ought to be. But such a hole can nowise stand with judgment and true sagacity, which Richard certainly has in a high degree. And it is very much to the point that, as in Lady Macbeth, his strength of will is evidently overstrained in keeping down the insurgent moral forces of his being. But this part of his nature asserts itself in his sleep, when his powers of self-repression are suspended: then his involuntary forces rise in insurrection against the despotism of his voluntary. In his speech to the army near the close, he describes conscience as " a word that cowards use, devised at first to keep the strong in awe "; and this well shows how hard he strives to hide from others, and even from himself, the workings of that deity in his breast: but the horrid dreams which infest his pillow and plague his slumbers, and which are disclosed to us by Lady Anne, are a conclusive record of the torturing thoughts that have long been rending and harrowing his inner man in his active career, and of the extreme violence his nature has suffered from the tyranny of will in repressing all outward signs of the work going on within. That his conscience in sleep should thus rouse itself and act the fury in his soul, to avenge the wrongs of his terrible self-despotism when awake, — this it is that, more than any thing else, vindicates his partnership in humanity, and keeps him within the circle of our human sympathies.

Richard's inexorable tenacity of purpose and his overbearing self-mastery have their strongest display in the catastrophe. He cannot indeed prolong his life; but he makes his death serve in the highest degree the end for which he has lived; dying in a perfect transport of heroism, insomuch that we may truly say, "nothing in his life became him like the leaving it." Nay, he may even be said to compel his own death, when a higher power than man's has cut off all other means of honour and triumph. Herein, too, the Poet followed the history: but in the prerogatives of his art he found out a way, which history knows not of, to satisfy the moral feelings; representing the hero as in Hands that can well afford to let him defy all the powers of human avengement. Inaccessible to earthly strokes, or accessible to them only in a way that adds to his earthly honour, yet this dreadful impunity is recompensed in the agonies of an embosomed hell; and our moral nature reaps a stern satisfaction in the retributions which are rendered vocal and articulate by the ghosts that are made to haunt his sleeping moments. For even so the Almighty sometimes chooses, apparently, to vindicate His law by taking the punishment directly and exclusively into His own hands. And, surely, His vengeance is never so awful as when subordinate ministries are thus dispensed with.

I here refer, of course, to what takes place the night before the battle of Bosworth-field. The matter was evidently suggested by the history, which gives it thus: "The fame went, that he had the same night a terrible dream; for it seemed to him, being asleep, that he did see divers images like terrible devils, which pulled and haled him, not

suffering him to take any rest. The which strange vision
not so suddenly strake his heart with fear, but it stuffed his
head with many busy and dreadful imaginations." The
effect of this vision is best told by Richard himself, when
he starts from his couch in an ecstasy of fright :

> Give me another horse ! bind up my wounds ! —
> Have mercy, Jesu ! — Soft ! I did but dream.
> O coward conscience, how dost thou afflict me ! —
> The lights burn blue.   It is now dead midnight.
> Cold fearful drops stand on my trembling flesh.
> My conscience hath a thousand several tongues,
> And every tongue brings in a several tale,
> And every tale condemns me for a villain.
> I shall despair.   There is no creature loves me ;
> And, if I die, no soul shall pity me.
>   *Rat.* [*Entering.*] My lord, —
>   *Rich.* Who's there ?
>   *Rat.* My lord, 'tis I.   The early village-cock
> Hath twice done salutation to the morn ;
> Your friends are up, and buckle on their armour.
>   *Rich.* O Ratcliff, I have dream'd a fearful dream !
> What thinkest thou, will our friends prove all true ?
>   *Rat.* No doubt, my lord.
>   *Rich.*   O Ratcliff, I fear, I fear !
> Methought the souls of all that I had murder'd
> Came to my tent ; and every one did threat
> To-morrow's vengeance on the head of Richard.
>   *Rat.* Nay, good my lord, be not afraid of shadows.
>   *Rich.* By the apostle Paul, shadows to-night
> Have struck more terror to the heart of Richard
> Than can the substance of ten thousand soldiers
> Armèd in proof and led by shallow Richmond.

Thus the still small voice, which Richard so tyrannically
strangles while consciousness is vigilant, takes its turn of
tyranny with him when his other forces are in abeyance.
And I suppose his intense, feverish activity of mind and
body when awake springs in part from the gnawings of the

worm : he endeavours, or rather is impelled, to stifle or lose the sense of guilt in a high-pressure stress and excitement of thought and work. For so the smothered pangs of remorse often act as potent stimulants or irritants of the intellect and will ; the hell within burning the fiercer for being repressed, and so heating the brain into restless, convulsive activity. In this way, the very conscience of crime may have the effect of plunging the subject into further crimes : Remorse

> Works in his guilty hopes and selfish fears,
> And, while she scares him, goads him to his fate.

And it is through the secret working of this power that Henry's prophecy touching Richmond, and also the fortune-teller's prediction which made the hero start on seeing the castle at Exeter, and hearing it called Rougemont, stick so fast in his memory, and sit so heavy on his soul through the closing struggle. As Gervinus says, "he who in his realistic free-thinking was fain to deny all higher powers, and by his hypocrisy to deceive even Heaven itself, succumbs at last to their inevitable stroke."

Character of Margaret.

The introduction of Margaret in this play has no formal warrant in history. After the battle of Tewksbury, May, 1471, she was confined in the Tower till 1475, when, being ransomed by her father, she went into France, and died there in 1482. So that the part she takes in these scenes is, throughout, a dramatic fiction. And a very judicious piece of fiction it is too. Nor is it without a basis of truth ; for, though absent in person, she was notwithstanding present in spirit, and in the memory of her voice, which seemed to be still ringing in the ears of both friends and foes. Her character, too, like Richard's, has its growth and shaping in the preceding plays of *King Henry the Sixth;* which makes it needful to revert to certain matters there presented.

Henry the Fifth had made great conquests in France, and died in 1422, leaving the crown to his infant son, afterwards Henry the Sixth, who at the age of twenty-two was married to Margaret of Anjou. During his nonage, what with the rising spirit of France, and what with the fierce feuds that sprang up amongst the English leaders, the provinces in France were recovered one after another to the French crown. The English people were vastly proud of those conquests, and were stung almost to madness at the loss of them. Hence grew the long series of civil wars known as "the Wars of the Roses." The great and fiery spirit of Margaret was present and active all through that conflict. The irritations caused by the losses in France are repre-sented by Shakespeare as so many eggs of discord in the nest of English life, and Margaret as the hot-breasted fury that hatched them into effect; her haughty, vindictive tem-per, her indomitable energy, and fire-spouting tongue fitting her to be, as indeed she was, a constant provoker and stirrer-up of hatreds and strifes.

Much has been said by one critic and another about the Poet's Lancastrian prejudices as manifested in this series of plays. One may well be curious to know whether those pre-judices are to be held responsible for the portrait he gives of Margaret, wherein we have, so to speak, an abbreviature and compendium of nearly all the worst vices of her time. The character, however lifelike and striking in its effect, is coloured much beyond what sober history warrants : though some of the main features are not without a basis of fact, still the composition and expression as a whole has hardly enough of historical truth to render it a caricature. A bold, ferocious, and tempestuous woman, void alike of delicacy, of dignity, and of discretion, all the bad passions out of which might be engendered the madness of civil war seem to flock and hover about her footsteps. Her speech and action, however, impart a wonderful vigour and lustihood to the scenes wherein she moves ; and perhaps it was only by exaggerating her, or some other person, into a sort of representative character, that the springs and processes of that long national bear-fight could be developed in a poetical or dramatic form. Her penetrating intellect and unrestrainable volubility discourse forth the motives and principles of the combantant factions ; while in her remorseless impiety and revengeful ferocity is impersonated, as it were, the very genius and spirit of the terrible conflict. So that we may regard her as, in some sort, an ideal concentration of that murderous ecstasy which seized upon the nation. And it should be observed withal, that popular tradition, sprung from the reports of her enemies, and cherished by patriotic feeling, had greatly overdrawn the wickedness of Margaret, to the end, apparently, that it might have something foreign whereon to father the evils resulting from her husband's weakness and the moral distemper of the times.

The dramatic character of Margaret, whether as transpiring at Court or in the field, is sustained at the same high pitch through all the plays wherein she figures. Afflictions do but open in her breast new founts of imbitterment : her speech is ever teeming with the sharp answer that engenders wrath ; and out of every wound issues the virulence that is sure to provoke another blow. If any one thinks that her ferocity is strained up to a pitch incompatible with her sex, and unnecessary for the occasion ; perhaps it will be deemed a sufficient answer, that the spirit of such a war could scarce be dramatically conveyed without the presence of a fury, and that the Furies have always been represented as females.

I will add a few words touching the reason which seems to have justified the Poet in carrying on the part of Margaret, against the literal truth of history, into the scenes of *King Richard the Third*.

Now it is considerable that in the earlier plays Richard is made several years older than he really was. Old enough, however, he was in fact, to have the spirit of the times thoroughly transfused into his character. There can be no doubt that the pungent seasoning sprinkled in here and there from the bad heart and busy brain of the precocious Richard is a material addition to those plays in an artistic point of view. But there was, I think, good cause in the substantial truth of things why Richard should be there just as he is. In point of moral history, it was but right to forecast the style of character which the proceedings then on foot were likely to generate and hand down to after-times. And as in the earlier plays Richard supplies such a forecast, so in the later play Margaret supplies a corresponding retrospect. She was continued on the scene, to the end, apparently, that the parties might have a terrible present remembrancer of their former deeds ; just as the manhood of Richard had been anticipated for the purpose, as would seem, of forecasting the final issues from the earlier stages of that multitudinous tragedy. So that there appears to be some reason in the ways of Providence, as well as in the laws of Art, why Margaret should still be kept in presence, as the fitting counterpart of that terrible man,—so merry-hearted, subtle-witted, and bloody-handed, whose mental efficacy turns perjury, murder, and what is worse, if aught worse there be, to poetry, — as he grows on from youth to manhood, and from manhood to his end, at once the offspring and the avenger of civil butchery.

As for the part which Margaret takes in the scenes of *King Richard the Third*, I have but little to add respecting it. Her condition is vastly different indeed from what it was in the earlier plays, but her character remains the same. She is here stripped of arms and instruments, so that her thoughts can no longer work out in acts. But, for this very cause, her Amazonian energies concentrate themselves so much the more in her speech; and her eloquence, while retaining all its strength and fluency, burns the deeper, forasmuch as it is the only organ of her mind that she has left. In brief, she is still the same high-grown, wide-branching tree, now rendered leafless indeed, and therefore all the fitter for the blasts of heaven to howl and whistle through! Long suffering has deepened her fierceness into sublimity. At once vindictive and broken-hearted, her part runs into a most impressive blending of the terrible and the pathetic. Walpole, in his *Historic Doubts*, remarks that in this play the Poet " seems to deduce the woes of the House of York from the curses which Queen Margaret had vented against them." Might it not as well be said that her woes are deduced from the curse formerly laid upon her by the Duke of York? I can perceive no deduction in either case : each seems but to have a foresight of future woe to the other, as the proper consequence of past or present crimes. The truth is, Margaret's curses do but proclaim those moral retributions of which God is the author, and Nature His minister ; and perhaps the only way her former character could be carried on into these scenes was by making her seek indemnity for *her* woes in ringing changes upon the woes of others. She is a sort of wailing or ululating chorus to the thick-thronging butcheries and agonies that wind their course through the play. A great, brave, fearful woman indeed, made sacred by all the anguishes that a wife and a mother can know !

Minor Characters.

Of the other characters in this play probably little need be said.— Hastings and Buckingham neither get nor deserve any pity from us. They have done all they could to nurse and prepare the human tiger that finally hunts them to death. Their thorough steeping in the wickedness of the times, and their reckless participation, either by act or by sympathy in Richard's slaughters, mark them out as worthy victims when, from motives no better than he is actuated by, they undertake to block the course which they have themselves exulted to see that living roll of hell-fire pursue.

Stanley gauges the hero rightly from the first, penetrates his closest designs, and then adroitly fathers the results of his own insight upon some current superstition of omens or dreams. Without sharing in any of Richard's crimes or defiling his hands at all with blood, he turns Richard's weapons against him, and fairly beats him at his own game.. His relationship to Richmond naturally marks him out for suspicion : he forecasts this from afar, and with a kind of honest knavery so shapes his course that he can easily parry or dodge or quiet the suspicion when it comes. With clean purposes, he dissembles them as completely as Richard does his foul ones. He is in secret correspondence with Richmond all along ; yet carries it so, that no wind thereof gets abroad. His art takes on the garb of perfect frankness, candour, and simplicity, which is art indeed. He counsels Dorset to speed his flight to Richmond, and gives him letters; then goes straight to Richard, and tells him Dorset has fled. He is also the first to inform Richard that "Richmond is on the seas," and that "he makes for England, here to claim the crown." By this timely speaking of what is true, but what he would naturally be least expected to disclose, he makes a passage for the full-grown deceit which he is presently forced to use. But he justly holds it a work of honesty to deceive such an arch-deceiver in such a cause. And his patriotism and rectitude of purpose are amply shown in that, when the crisis comes, he stakes what is dearest in the world to him, for the deliverance of his country from the butchering tyrant. This was a good beginning for the noble and illustrious House of Stanley, which has, I believe, in all ages since stood true alike to loyalty and liberty.

The parts of Lady Anne, of Elizabeth, the Duchess of York, and the two young Princes, are skilfully managed so as to diversify and relieve what would else be a prolonged monotony of atrocious wickedness and intellectual circus-riding. I say relieve, for the change from the society of such consummate hypocrisies and villainies to that of heart-rending sorrow is a relief: nay, it is almost a positive happiness thus to escape now and then from the doers of wrong, and breathe awhile with the sufferers of wrong.

Lady Anne's seeming levity in yielding to the serpent flatteries of the wooing homicide is readily forgiven in the sore burden of grief which it entails upon her, in her subdued gentleness to other destined victims, and in the sad resignation with which she forecasts the bitterness of her brief future.

Her nature is felt to be all too soft to stand against the crafty and merciless tormentor into whose hand she has given herself; and she seems

> Like a poor bird entangled in a snare,
> Whose heart still flutters, though her wings forbear
> To stir in useless struggle.

Elizabeth is prudent, motherly, and pitiful, withal by no means lacking in strength and spirit. Stanley, Margaret, and the Duchess excepted, she is the only person in the play who reads correctly the hero's character. From the slaughter of her kindred at Pomfret, her instinctive feminine sagacity gathers at once the whole scheme of what is coming, and anticipates the utter ruin of her House. But she is so benetted round with intriguing arts, and, what is still worse, so beset with the friendly assurances of minds less penetrating than hers, that all her defences prove of no avail in the chief point. It was both wise and kind in the Poet to represent her voice as so untuned to the language of imprecation, that she has to call on one so eloquent in curses as Margaret to do her cursing for her. In the scene where Richard wooes so persistently for her daughter's hand, it appears something uncertain whether she is really beguiled and won by his wizard rhetoric, or whether she only temporizes, and feigns a reluctant acquiescence, and so at last fairly outwits him. Most critics, I believe, have taken the former view; but I am far from seeing it so: for her daughter's hand is firmly pledged to Richmond already, and she is in the whole secret of the plot for seating him on the throne. So I take it as an instance of that profound yet innocent and almost unconscious guile which women are apt to use in defence of those they love, and which so often proves an overmatch for all the resources of deliberate craft.

The two Princes are charmingly discriminated, and the delineation of them, though compressed into a few brief speeches, is an exquisite piece of work. The elder is inquisitive, thoughtful, cautious in his words, hardly knowing whether to fear his uncle or not, and, with a fine instinctive tact, veiling his doubt under a pregnant equivoque. The younger is pert, precocious, and clever, and prattles out his keen childish wit, in perfect freedom from apprehension, and quite innocent of the stings it carries. Their guileless intelligence and sweet trustfulness of disposition make a capital foil to the Satanic subtlety and virulent intellectuality of Richard.

General Remarks.

This drama has, in my judgment, many and great faults, some of which I have noted already. Certain scenes and passages excepted, the workmanship in all its parts, in language, structure of the verse, and quality of tone, is greatly below what we find in the Poet's later plays. In many places, there is an overstudied roundness of diction and regularity of movement; therewithal the persons often deliver themselves too much in the style of set speeches, and rather as authors striving for effect than as men and women stirred by the real passions and interests of life; there is at times an artificial and bookish tang in the dialogue, and many strains of elaborate jingle made by using the same word in different senses: all smacking as if the Poet wrote more from what he had read in books, or heard at the theatre, than from what his most prying, quick, and apprehensive ear had caught of the unwritten drama of actual and possible men. In illustration

of the point, I may aptly refer to the hero's soliloquy when
he starts so wildly from his "fearful dream"; some parts of
which are in or near the Poet's best style, others in his worst.
The good parts I have quoted already, and those are indeed
good enough : the rest is made up of forced conceits and
affectations, such as Nature utterly refuses to own ; albeit
the plays and novels of that time were generally full of them.
Here is a brief specimen :

> What do I fear ? myself ? there's none else by :
> Richard loves Richard ; that is, I am I.
> Is there a murderer here ? No ; — yes, I am :
> Then fly. What, from myself ? Great reason why, —
> Lest I revenge myself upon myself.
> Alack, I love myself. Wherefore ? for any good
> That I myself have done unto myself ?
> O, no ! alas, I rather hate myself
> For hateful deeds committed by myself.

It is hard to believe that Shakespeare could have written this
at any time of his life, or that the speaker was meant to be
in earnest in twisting such riddles ; but he was. Some have
indeed claimed to see a reason for the thing in the speaker's
state of mind ; but this view is, to my thinking, quite upset
by the better parts of the same speech.

On the whole, then, I should say that in this piece the
author is struggling and vibrating between the native impulses
of his genius and the force of custom and example ; or like
one just passing out of youth into manhood, and fluctuating
between the two. For even so, in some of his plays, the
Poet seems going more by fashion than by inspiration, or con-
sulting now what is within him, now what is around him. And
I think it stands to reason, that he could not have reached
his own high ways of art without first practising in the ways
already open and approved. Of course, as experience grad-

ually developed his native strength, and at the same time taught him what this was sufficient for, he would naturally throw aside more and more the aids of custom and precedent ; since these would come to be felt as incumbrances in proportion as he grew able to do better without them.

And this would naturally hold much more in his efforts at tragedy than at comedy. For the elements of comedy, besides being more light and wieldy in themselves, had been playing freely about his boyhood, and mingling in his earliest observation of human life and character : so that here he would be apt to cast himself more quickly and unreservedly upon Nature, as he had been used to meet and converse with her. Tragedy, on the other hand, must in all reason have been to him a much more artificial thing ; and he would needs require both a larger measure and a stronger faculty of observation and experience, before he could find the elements of it in Nature, and become able to digest and modulate them into the many-toned yet severe and nicely-balanced harmony of Dramatic Art. Is it not clear, then, that in proportion as he lacked the power to grasp and wield the forces of tragedy, in his first efforts in that kind, he would be mainly governed by what stood before him, and that the adventitious helps and influences of the time would be prominently reproduced in his work? Therefore it is, no doubt, that his earlier comedies are so much more Shakespearian in style and spirit and characterization than his tragedies of the same period. For can it be questioned that such a man so circumstanced would both *find himself* and make others find him sooner in comedy than in tragedy? At all events, it is certain that his earlier labours in both kinds were, to a great extent, specimens of imitation ; though, indeed, of imitation surpassing its models. It seems in fact to have been through the process of imitation that his character and idiom got worked out into free and self-reliant action.

So that, as I have elsewhere remarked, it is a great mistake to regard Shakespeare as one with whom the ordinary laws and methods of intellectual growth and virtue had little or nothing to do. He must indeed have been a prodigious infant; yet an infant he unquestionably was; and had to proceed by the usual paths from infancy to manhood, however unusual may have been the ease and speed of his passage. Dowered perhaps with such a portion of genius as hath fallen to no other mortal, still his powers had to struggle through the common infirmities and incumbrances of our nature. For, assuredly, his mighty mind was not born full-grown and ready-furnished for the course and service of Truth, but had to creep, totter, and prattle; much study, observation, experience, in a word, a long, severe *tentative* process being required to insinew and discipline and regulate his genius into power.

KING RICHARD THE THIRD.

PERSONS REPRESENTED.

KING EDWARD THE FOURTH.
EDWARD, Prince of Wales, } his Sons.
RICHARD, Duke of York, }
Duke of Clarence, } his Brothers.
Duke of Gloster, }
A young Son of Clarence.
HENRY TUDOR, Earl of Richmond.
BOURCHIER, Primate of England.
ROTHERHAM, Archbishop of York.
JOHN MORTON, Bishop of Ely.
STAFFORD, Duke of Buckingham.
JOHN HOWARD, Duke of Norfolk.
THOMAS, his Son, Earl of Surrey.
WOODVILLE, Earl Rivers.
Marquess of Dorset, } Sons of the
RICHARD LORD GREY, } Queen.
JOHN DE VERE, Earl of Oxford.
WILLIAM LORD HASTINGS.
THOMAS LORD STANLEY.

FRANCIS LORD LOVEL.
Sir THOMAS VAUGHAN.
Sir RICHARD RATCLIFF.
Sir WILLIAM CATESBY.
Sir JAMES TYRREL.
Sir WILLIAM BRANDON.
Sir JAMES BLUNT.
Sir WALTER HERBERT.
Sir ROBERT BRAKENBURY.
CHRISTOPHER URSWICK, a Priest.
Another Priest.
Lord Mayor of London.
Sheriff of Wiltshire.

ELIZABETH, Queen of Edward IV.
MARGARET, Widow of Henry VI.
CECILY, Duchess of York.
LADY ANNE.
A young Daughter of Clarence.

Lords and other Attendants; two Gentlemen, a Pursuivant, Scrivener, Citizens, Murderers, Messengers, Ghosts, Soldiers, &c.

SCENE. — *England.*

ACT I.

SCENE I. — *London.   A Street.*

Enter GLOSTER.

Glos. Now is the Winter of our discontent
Made glorious Summer by this sun,[1] of York;

[1] The cognizance of Edward IV. was *a sun*, in memory of the three suns

And all the clouds that lour'd upon our House
In the deep bosom of the ocean buried.
Now are our brows bound with victorious wreaths;
Our bruisèd arms hung up for monuments;
Our stern alarums changed to merry meetings,
Our dreadful marches to delightful measures.[2]
Grim-visaged war hath smooth'd his wrinkled front;
And now — instead of mounting barbèd[3] steeds
To fright the souls of fearful[4] adversaries —
He capers nimbly in a lady's chamber
To the lascivious pleasing of a lute.
But I, that am not shaped for sportive tricks,
Nor made to court an amorous looking-glass;
I, that am rudely stamp'd, and want love's majesty
To strut before a wanton ambling nymph;
I, that am cúrtail'd of this fair proportion,[5]
Cheated of feature by dissembling Nature,[6]

which are said to have appeared at the battle he gained over the Lancastrians at Mortimer's Cross. See Third Part of *Henry the Sixth*, ii. 1.

[2] *Measure* was the name of a *dance*. See *Much Ado*, page 42, note 5.

[3] *Barbed* is *caparisoned* or *clothed* in the trappings of war. The word is properly *barded*, from equus *bardatus*.

[4] *Fearful* was, as it still is, used in the two opposite senses of *terrible* and *timorous*. Here it probably has the former.

[5] *Proportion* for *form*, *shape*, or *personal aspect*. Repeatedly so. "This fair proportion" may refer to what has just been spoken of as "love's majesty." But *this* is probably here used indefinitely, and with something of a sneer. The demonstrative pronouns were, and still are, often used thus. So in *2 Henry IV.*, i. 2 : "*This* apoplexy is, as I take it, a kind of lethargy."

[6] *Feature* in the sense of *form* or *figure*, and referring to the person in general. So in More's description of Richard : "Little of stature, *ill-featured of limbs*, crook-backed." — *Dissembling*, here, is sometimes explained to mean, not *deceiving*, but putting together or *assembling* things not *semblable*, as a brave mind and a deformed body. It may be so; but the word *cheated* seems to make rather strongly against this explanation.

Deform'd, unfinish'd, sent before my time
Into this breathing world, scarce half made up,
And that so lamely and unfashionable,
That dogs bark at me as I halt by them ; —
Why, I, in this weak piping time of peace,
Have no delight to pass away the time,
Unless to spy my shadow in the sun,
And descant on mine own deformity :
And therefore — since I cannot prove a lover,
To entertain these fair well-spoken days —
I am determinéd to prove a villain,
And hate the idle pleasures of these days.
Plots have I laid, inductions [7] dangerous,
By drunken prophecies, libels, and dreams,
To set my brother Clarence and the King
In deadly hate the one against the other :
And, if King Edward be as true and just
As I am subtle, false, and treacherous,
This day should Clarence closely be mew'd up,[8]
About a prophecy, which says that G
Of Edward's heirs the murderer shall be.
Dive, thoughts, down to my soul : here Clarence comes. —

Enter CLARENCE, *guarded, and* BRAKENBURY.

Brother, good day : what means this armèd guard
That waits upon your Grace ?
    Clar.   His Majesty,

---

  [7] *Inductions* are beginnings, preparations ; things that draw on or *induce*
events. Shakespeare has the word just so in two other places.

  [8] To *mew up* was a term in falconry ; hawks being shut up or confined in
a *mew* during the season of moulting.

Tendering [9] my person's safety, hath appointed
This conduct [10] to convey me to the Tower.

   Glos. Upon what cause?

   Clar.   Because my name is George.

   Glos. Alack, my lord, that fault is none of yours;
He should, for that, commit your godfathers:
O, belike his Majesty hath some intent
That you shall be new-christen'd in the Tower.
But what's the matter, Clarence? may I know?

   Clar. Yea, Richard, when I know; for I protest
As yet I do not: but, as I can learn,
He hearkens after prophecies and dreams;
And from the cross-row [11] plucks the letter G,
And says a wizard told him that by G
His issue disinherited should be;
And, for [12] my name of George begins with G,
It follows in his thought that I am he.
These, as I learn, and such-like toys [13] as these,
Have moved his Highness to commit me now.

   Glos. Why, this it is, when men are ruled by women:
'Tis not the King that sends you to the Tower;
My Lady Grey his wife, Clarence, 'tis she

---

   [9] To *tender* a thing is to be *careful* of it, to have a *tender regard* for it, to *hold it dear*. See *Hamlet*, page 73, note 27.

   [10] *Conduct* for *conductor*, or *escort*. See *Twelfth Night*, p. 105, note 20.

   [11] *Cross-row* is an abbreviation of *Christ-cross-row*, and means the *alphabet*, which is said to have been so called, either because a cross was placed before it, or because it was written in the form of a cross, to be used as a sort of charm.

   [12] *For* is here equivalent to *because;* a frequent usage.

   [13] *Toys* for *whims, fancies,* or *freaks of imagination.* So in *Hamlet*, i. 4·
"The very place puts *toys* of desperation into every brain that looks so many fathoms to the sea," &c.

That tempers [14] him to this extremity.
Was it not she, and that good man of worship,
Antony Woodeville,[15] her brother there,
That made him send Lord Hastings to the Tower,
From whence this present day he is deliver'd?
We are not safe, Clarence ; we are not safe.

Clar. By Heaven, I think there is no man secure
But the Queen's kindred, and night-walking heralds
That trudge betwixt the King and Mistress Shore.
Heard ye not what an humble suppliant
Lord Hastings was to her for his delivery?

Glos. Humbly complaining to her Deity
Got my Lord Chamberlain his liberty.
I'll tell you what ; I think it is our way,
If we will keep in favour with the King,
To be her men, and wear her livery :
The jealous o'erworn widow and herself,[16]
Since that our brother dubb'd them gentlewomen,
Are mighty gossips in this monarchy.

Brak. Beseech your Graces both to pardon me ;
His Majesty hath straitly given in charge
That no man shall have private conference,
Of what degree soever, with his brother.

Glos. Even so ; an please your Worship, Brakenbury,
You may partake of any thing we say :
We speak no treason, man : we say the King

---

14 *Tempers* is *frames, fashions,* or *disposes.*

15 This name is here three syllables.   Commonly spelt *Woodville.*

16 The *widow* is Queen Elizabeth, the name of whose deceased husband
was Grey.   *Herself* refers to Mrs. Jane Shore, quite a noted character of
the time, whom King Edward is said to have cherished as a sort of left-hand
wife.   She was much mixed up with the intrigues of the Court.

Is wise and virtuous ; and his noble Queen
Well struck in years, fair, and not jealous :
We say that Shore's wife hath a pretty foot,
A cherry lip, a bonny eye, a passing pleasing tongue ;
And the Queen's kindred are made gentlefolks :
How say you, sir ? can you deny all this ?

 Brak. With this, my lord, myself have nought to do.

 Glos. Nought to do with Mistress Shore ! I tell thee, fellow,
He that doth naught [17] with her, excepting one,
Were best to do it secretly, alone.

 Brak. What one, my lord ?

 Glos. Her husband, knave : wouldst thou betray me ?

 Brak. Beseech your Grace to pardon me ; and, withal,
Forbear your conference with the noble duke.

 Clar. We know thy charge, Brakenbury, and will obey.

 Glos. We are the Queen's abjects,[18] and must obey.—
Brother, farewell : I will unto the King ;
And whatsoe'er you will employ me in,—
Were it to call King Edward's widow sister,—
I will perform it to enfranchise you.
Meantime, this deep disgrace in brotherhood
Touches me deeper than you can imagine.

 Clar. I know it pleaseth neither of us well.

 Glos. Well, your imprisonment shall not be **long** ;
I will deliver you, or else lie for you : [19]
Meantime have patience.

---

[17] Richard is quibbling between *nought* and *naught*, the latter of which
has the sense of *bad*, as in our word *naughty*.

[18] The lowest of her subjects. This substantive is found in Psalm xxxv.
15 : "Yea, the very *abjects* came together against me unawares, making
mouths at me, and ceased not."

[19] Or else *lie in prison* in your stead. But a quibble is probably intended
between the two senses of *lie*.

Clar.   I must perforce : farewell.
[*Exeunt* CLARENCE, BRAKENBURY, *and Guard.*

Glos. Go, tread the path that thou shalt ne'er return,
Simple, plain Clarence !   I do love thee so,
That I will shortly send thy soul to Heaven,
If Heaven will take the present at our hands.
But who comes here? the new-deliver'd Hastings?

Enter HASTINGS.

Hast. Good time of day unto my gracious lord !
Glos. As much unto my good Lord Chamberlain !
Well are you welcome to the open air.
How hath your lordship brook'd imprisonment?
Hast. With patience, noble lord, as prisoners must :
But I shall live, my lord, to give them thanks
That were the cause of my imprisonment.
Glos. No doubt, no doubt; and so shall Clarence too ;
For they that were your enemies are his,
And have prevail'd as much on [20] him as you.
Hast. More pity that the eagle should be mew'd,
While kites and buzzards prey at liberty.
Glos. What news abroad?
Hast. No news so bad abroad as this at home :
The King is sickly, weak, and melancholy,
And his physicians fear him [21] mightily.
Glos. Now, by Saint Paul,[22] this news is bad indeed.
O, he hath kept an evil diet long,
And overmuch consumed his royal person :

---

[20] *Prevail'd on* is here used for *prevail'd against.*

[21] Fear *for* him, of course. This mode of speech was not uncommon.
See *The Merchant,* page 157, note 1.

[22] " By Saint Paul " was in fact Richard's favourite oath.

'Tis very grievous to be thought upon.
What, is he in his bed?

 Hast. He is.

 Glos. Go you before, and I will follow you.—

           [*Exit* HASTINGS.

He cannot live, I hope; and must not die
Till George be pack'd with post-haste up to Heaven.
I'll in, to urge his hatred more to Clarence,
With lies well steel'd with weighty arguments;
And, if I fail not in my deep intent,
Clarence hath not another day to live:
Which done, God take King Edward to His mercy,
And leave the world for me to bustle in!
For then I'll marry Warwick's youngest daughter:[23]
What though I kill'd her husband and her father?
The readiest way to make the wench amends,
Is to become her husband and her father:
The which will I; not all so much for love
As for another secret close intent,[24]
By marrying her which I must reach unto.
But yet I run before my horse to market:
Clarence still breathes; Edward still lives and reigns:
When they are gone, then must I count my gains. [*Exit.*

---

[23] This was Lady Anne, daughter of Richard Neville, the great Earl of Warwick, known in history as the "king-maker." She had been married to Edward, Prince of Wales, son of King Henry the Sixth. Her young husband was killed, murdered, it was said, at the battle of Tewksbury, which took place May 4th, 1471. Her oldest sister, Isabella, wife to the Clarence of this play, had died some time before.

[24] This "secret close intent" probably was to get into his hands the son and daughter of Clarence, who had been left in the care of Lady Anne their aunt, and had succeeded to the larger portion of the vast estates of their grandfather, the great Earl of Warwick.

SCENE II. — *The Same.   Another Street.*

Enter the corpse of King HENRY *the Sixth, borne in an open coffin,* Gentlemen *with halberds to guard it,* — *among them* TRESSEL *and* BERKELEY ; *and Lady* ANNE *as Mourner.*

Anne. Set down, set down your honourable load, —
If honour may be shrouded in a hearse, —
Whilst I awhile obsequiously[1] lament
Th' untimely fall of virtuous Lancaster. —

                         [*The Bearers set down the coffin.*

Poor key-cold[2] figure of a holy king !
Pale ashes of the House of Lancaster !
Thou bloodless remnant of that royal blood !
Be 't lawful that I invocate thy ghost
To hear the lamentations of poor Anne,
Wife to thy Edward, to thy slaughter'd son,
Stabb'd by the selfsame hand that made these wounds !
Lo, in these windows that let forth thy life,
I pour the helpless balm of my poor eyes :
O, cursèd be the hand that made these holes !
Cursèd the heart that had the heart to do it !
Cursèd the blood that let this blood from hence !
More direful hap betide that hated wretch
That makes us wretched by the death of thee,

---

[1] To lament *obsequiously* is to make the lamentation proper to *obsequies,* or rites of burial. See *Hamlet,* page 60, note 21.

[2] As *cold* as a *key;* but why a key should be taken for an image of coldness is not very clear. The usage is not uncommon in the old writers. Shakespeare has it again in *Lucrece:* "And then in *key-cold* Lucrece' bleeding stream he falls." Thus, also, in Holland's Pliny : "In this habite, disguised as hee sat, hee was starke dead and *key-cold* before any man perceived it."

Than I can wish to adders, spiders, toads,
Or any creeping venom'd thing that lives !
If ever he have child, abortive be it,
Prodigious,[3] and untimely brought to light,
Whose ugly and unnatural aspéct
May fright the hopeful mother at the view ;
And that be heir to his unhappiness ![4]
If ever he have wife, let her be made
More miserable by the death of him
Than I am made by my young lord and thee ! —
Come, now towards Chertsey with your holy load,
Taken from Paul's to be interrèd there ;
And still, as you are weary of the weight,
Rest you, whiles I lament King Henry's corse.

       [The Bearers take up the coffin and move forwards.

Enter GLOSTER.

  Glos. Stay, you that bear the corse, and set it down.

  Anne. What black magician conjures up this fiend,
To stop devoted charitable deeds ?

  Glos. Villains, set down the corse ; or, by Saint Paul,
I'll make a corse of him that disobeys !

  1 Gent. My lord, stand back, and let the coffin pass.

  Glos. Unmanner'd dog ! stand thou, when I command :
Advance[5] thy halberd higher than my breast,
Or, by Saint Paul, I'll strike thee to my foot,

   [3] *Prodigious* for *monstrous ;* one of the Latin senses of the word. Such births were held to be of evil omen. See *A Midsummer-Night's Dream*, page 112, note 25.

   [4] *Unhappiness* here means *mischievousness*, or *propensity to mischief.* The Poet has it several times in this sense. See *Much Ado*, p. 53, note 32.

   [5] Here, as often, *advance* is *raise* or *lift up.* — *Unmanner'd*, in the preceding line, is *unmannerly*, or *insolent.*

And spurn upon thee, beggar, for thy boldness.

> [*The Bearers set down the coffin.*

Anne. What, do you tremble? are you all afraid?
Alas, I blame you not; for you are mortal,
And mortal eyes cannot endure the Devil. —
Avaunt, thou dreadful minister of Hell!
Thou hadst but power over his mortal body,
His soul thou canst not have; therefore be gone.

Glos. Sweet saint, for charity, be not so curst.[6]

Anne. Foul devil, for God's sake, hence, and trouble us not;
For thou hast made the happy Earth thy hell,
Fill'd it with cursing cries and deep exclaims.
If thou delight to view thy heinous deeds,
Behold this pattern of thy butcheries. —
O, gentlemen, see, see! dead Henry's wounds
Open their congeal'd mouths and bleed[7] afresh! —
Blush, blush, thou lump of foul deformity;
For 'tis thy presence that exhales[8] this blood
From cold and empty veins, where no blood dwells:
Thy deed, inhuman and unnatural,
Provokes this deluge most unnatural. —
O God, which this blood madest, revenge his death!
O Earth, which this blood drink'st, revenge his death!

---

[6] *Curst* is *sharp-tongued,* or fierce and bitter of speech. Repeatedly so. See *A Midsummer-Night's Dream,* page 77, note 26.

[7] This is founded on Holinshed's account of Henry's funeral: "The dead corps was conveied from the Tower to the church of saint Paule, and there laid on a beire or coffen bare-faced: the same in presence of the beholders *did bleed.* From thense he was caried to the Blackfriers, and *bled there* likewise." — It used to be thought that the body of a murdered person would bleed afresh, if touched or approached by the murderer.

[8] Shakespeare repeatedly has *exhale* in the sense of *draw out.* In *Henry V.* Pistol uses it imperatively, meaning, "draw thy sword."

Either, Heaven, with lightning strike the murderer dead;
Or, Earth, gape open wide, and eat him quick,[9]
As thou dost swallow up this good King's blood,
Which his hell-govern'd arm hath butcheréd!

Glos. Lady, you know no rules of charity,
Which renders good for bad, blessings for curses.

Anne. Villain, thou know'st no law of God nor man:
No beast so fierce but knows some touch of pity.

Glos. But I know none, and therefore am no beast.

Anne. O wonderful, when devils tell the truth!

Glos. More wonderful, when angels are so angry.
Vouchsafè, divine perfection of a woman,
Of these supposèd crimes, to give me leave,
By circumstance, but to acquit myself.

Anne. Vouchsafe, diffused[10] infection of a man,
For these known evils, but to give me leave,
By circumstance, to curse thy cursèd self.

Glos. Fairer than tongue can name thee, let me have
Some patient leisure to excuse myself.

Anne. Fouler than heart can think thee, thou canst make
No éxcuse current, but to hang thyself.

Glos. By such despair, I should accuse myself.

Anne. And, by despairing, shouldst thou stand excused
For doing worthy vengeance on thyself,
That didst unworthy slaughter upon others.

Glos. Say, that I slew them not.

Anne.   Why, then they are not dead:
But dead they are, and, devilish slave, by thee.

---

[9] *Quick* is *alive* or *living;* so that the meaning is *swallow* him alive. So in *Hamlet*, v. 1: "Be buried *quick* with her, and so will I." See, also, *The Winter's Tale*, page 117, note 18.

[10] *Diffused* sometimes meant *dark, obscure, uncouth,* or *confused.*

Glos. I did not kill your husband.

Anne.   Why, then he is alive.

Glos. Nay, he is dead; and slain by Edward's hand.

Anne. In thy foul throat thou liest: Queen Margaret saw
Thy murderous falchion smoking in his blood;
The which thou once didst bend against her breast,
But that thy brothers beat aside the point.

Glos. I was provokèd by her slanderous tongue,
That laid their guilt [11] upon my guiltless shoulders.

Anne. Thou wast provokèd by thy bloody mind,
That never dreamt on aught but butcheries:
Didst thou not kill this King?

Glos.   I grant ye.

Anne. Dost grant me, hedgehog? then, God grant me too
Thou mayst be damnèd for that wicked deed!
O, he was gentle, mild, and virtuous!

Glos. The fitter for the King of Heaven, that hath him.

Anne. He is in Heaven, where thou shalt never come.

Glos. Let him thank me, that holp [12] to send him thither;
For he was fitter for that place than Earth.

Anne. And thou unfit for any place but Hell.

Glos. Yes, one place else, if you will hear me name it.

Anne. Some dungeon.

Glos.   Your bed-chamber.

Anne. Ill rest betide the chamber where thou liest!

Glos. So will it, madam, till I lie with you.

Anne. I hope so.

Glos.   I know so. But, gentle Lady Anne, —

---

11 The guilt of his brothers who slew the Prince.

12 *Holp* or *holpen* is the old preterite form of the verb to *help*. It occurs
very often in the English *Psalter*, which is a much older version of the
Psalms than that in the Bible.

To leave this keen encounter of our wits,
And fall somewhát into a slower method, —
Is not the causer of the timeless [13] deaths
Of these Plantagenets, Henry and Edward,
As blameful as the executioner?

    Anne. Thou wast the cause, and most accursed th' effect.[14]

    Glos. Your beauty was the cause of that effect;
Your beauty that did haunt me in my sleep
To undertake the death of all the world,
So I might live one hour in your sweet bosom.

    Anne. If I thought that, I tell thee, homicide,
These nails should rend that beauty from my cheeks.

    Glos. These eyes could not endure that beauty's wreck;
You should not blemish it, if I stood by:
As all the world is cheerèd by the Sun,
So I by that; it is my day, my life.

    Anne. Black night o'ershade thy day, and death thy life!

    Glos. Curse not thyself, fair creature; thou art both.

    Anne. I would I were, to be revenged on thee.

    Glos. It is a quarrel most unnatural,
To be revenged on him that loveth thee.

    Anne. It is a quarrel just and reasonable,
To be revenged on him that kill'd my husband.

    Glos. He that bereft thee, lady, of thy husband,
Did it to help thee to a better husband.

    Anne. His better doth not breathe upon the Earth.

    Glos. He lives that loves thee better than he could.

---

[13] *Timeless*, here, is *untimely*. A frequent use of the word in Shakespeare's time. So in *Romeo and Juliet*, v. 3: "Poison, I see, hath been his *timeless* end." In the first speech of this scene, we have a like use of *helpless* for *unhelping* or *unavailing*: "I pour the *helpless* balm of my poor eyes."

[14] And most accursed *is the* effect; *effect* referring to *their death*.

Anne. Name him.

Glos.   Plantagenet.

Anne.   Why, that was he.

Glos. The selfsame name, but one of better nature.

Anne. Where is he?

Glos.   Here. [*She spits at him.*] Why dost
thou spit at me?

Anne. Would it were mortal poison, for thy sake!

Glos. Never came poison from so sweet a place.

Anne. Never hung poison on a fouler toad.
Out of my sight! thou dost infect mine eyes.

Glos. Thine eyes, sweet lady, have infected mine.

Anne. Would they were basilisks,[15] to strike thee dead!

Glos. I would they were, that I might die at once;
For now they kill me with a living death.
Those eyes of thine from mine have drawn salt tears,
Shamed their aspécts with store of childish drops:
These eyes, which never shed remorseful[16] tear, —
Not when my father York and Edward wept
To hear[17] the piteous moan that Rutland made
When black-faced Clifford shook his sword at him;
Nor when thy warlike father, like a child,
Told the sad story of my father's death,
And twenty times made pause to sob and weep,

---

[15] The Poet has several allusions to this imaginary power of the reptile, called *basilisk* from its having on the head some resemblance to a crown; the name being from the Greek, and signifying a little king. So Bacon, *Advancement of Learning*, xxi. 9: "For, as the fable goeth of the basilisk, that if he see you first, you die for it; but if you see him first, he dieth; so is it with deceits and evil arts." See *The Winter's Tale*, page 58, note 51.

[16] *Remorse* was continually used for *pity*, *remorseful* for *pitiful*.

[17] Wept *at hearing;* the infinitive used gerundively. The Poet abounds in this usage. See *Julius Cæsar*, page 137, note 2.

That all the standers-by had wet their cheeks,
Like trees bedash'd with rain ;— in that sad time
My manly eyes did scorn an humble tear ;
And what these sorrows could not thence exhale,
Thy beauty hath, and made them blind with weeping.
I never sued to friend nor enemy ;
My tongue could never learn sweet smoothing words ;
But, now thy beauty is proposed my fee,
My proud heart sues, and prompts my tongue to speak.
                    [*She looks scornfully at him.*
Teach not thy lips such scorn ; for they were made
For kissing, lady, not for such contempt.
If thy revengeful heart cannot forgive,
Lo, here I lend thee this sharp-pointed sword ;
Which if thou please to hide in this true breast,
And let the soul forth that adoreth thee,
I lay it naked to the deadly stroke,
And humbly beg the death upon my knee.
        [*Gives her his sword, and lays his breast open, kneeling.*
Nay, do not pause ; for I did kill King Henry,—
                [*She offers at his breast with his sword.*
But 'twas thy beauty that provokèd me.
Nay, now dispatch ; 'twas I that stabb'd young Edward,—
                    [*She again offers at his breast.*
But 'twas thy heavenly face that set me on.
                    [*She lets fall the sword.*
Take up the sword again, or take up me.
    Anne. Arise, dissembler : though I wish thy death,
I will not be thy executioner.
    Glos. Then bid me kill myself, and I will do it.
                    [*Rises, and takes up his sword.*
    Anne. I have already.

Glos.   That was in thy rage :
Speak it again, and, even with the word,
This hand, which for thy love did kill thy love,
Shall for thy love kill a far truer love ;
To both their deaths shalt thou be accessary.

 Anne. I would I knew thy heart.

 Glos. 'Tis figured in my tongue.

 Anne. I fear me both are false.

 Glos. Then never man was true.

 Anne. Well, well, put up your sword.

 Glos. Say, then, my peace is made.

 Anne. That shalt thou know hereafter.

 Glos. But shall I live in hope?

 Anne. All men, I hope, live so.

 Glos. Vouchsafe to wear this ring.

 Anne. To take, is not to give.   [*She puts on the ring.*

 Glos. Look, how my ring encompasseth thy finger,
Even so thy breast encloseth my poor heart ;
Wear both of them, for both of them are thine.
And, if thy poor devoted servant may
But beg one favour at thy gracious hand,
Thou dost confirm his happiness for ever.

 Anne. What is it?

 Glos. That it may please you leave these sad designs
To him that hath more cause to be a mourner,
And presently repair to Crosby-place ;
Where — after I have solemnly interr'd,
At Chertsey monastery, this noble King,
And wet his grave with my repentant tears —
I will with all expedient[18] duty see you :

  [18] *Expedient* for *expeditious.* Repeatedly so. So in *King John*, ii. 1:
" His marches are *expedient* to this town."

For divers unknown reasons, I beseech you,
Grant me this boon.

 Anne. With all my heart; and much it joys me too
To see you are become so penitent. —
Tressel and Berkeley, go along with me.

 Glos. Bid me farewell.

 Anne.   'Tis more than you deserve;
But, since you teach me how to flatter you,
Imagine I have said farewell already.

   [*Exeunt Lady* ANNE, TRESSEL, *and* BERKELEY.

 Glos. Sirs, take up the corse.

 Gent.   Towards Chertsey, noble lord?

 Glos. No, to White-Friars; there attend [19] my coming. —

   [*Exeunt all but* GLOSTER.

Was ever woman in this humour woo'd?
Was ever woman in this humour won?
I'll have her; — but I will not keep her long.
What! I, that kill'd her husband and his father,
To take her in her heart's extremest hate;
With curses in her mouth, tears in her eyes,
The bleeding witness of her hatred by;
Having God, her conscience, and these bars against me,
And I no friends to back my suit withal
But the plain devil and dissembling looks,
And yet to win her, — all the world to nothing! [20]
Ha!
Hath she forgot already that brave Prince,
Edward, her lord, whom I, some three months since,
Stabb'd in my angry mood at Tewksbury? [21]

---

[19] Here, as often, *attend* is *wait for* or *await*. So in *Coriolanus*, **i. 1:**
" Your company to th' Capitol; where our greatest friends *attend* us!"

 [20] " The chances against me were as all the world to nothing."

 [21] This fixes the time of the scene to August, 1471. King Edward, how-

A sweeter and a lovelier gentleman —
Framed in the prodigality of Nature,
Young, wise, and valiant, and, no doubt, right royal —
The spacious world cannot again afford :
And will she yet abase [22] her eyes on me,
That cropp'd the golden prime of this sweet Prince,
And made her widow to a woeful bed ?
On me, whose all not equals Edward's moiety ?
On me, that halt and am mis-shapen thus ?
My dukedom to a beggarly denier,[23]
I do mistake my person all this while :
Upon my life, she finds, although I cannot,
Myself to be a marvellous proper [24] man.
I'll be at charges for a looking-glass ;
And entertain a score or two of tailors
To study fashions to adorn my body :
Since I am crept in favour with myself,
I will maintain it with some little cost.
But first I'll turn yon fellow in [25] his grave ;
And then return lamenting to my love. —
Shine out, fair Sun, till I have bought a glass,
That I may see my shadow as I pass.   [*Exit.*

ever, is introduced in the second Act dying. That King died in April,
1483; consequently there is an interval between this Act and the next of
almost twelve years. Clarence, who is represented in the preceding scene
as committed to the Tower before the burial of King Henry VI., was in fact
not confined till February, 1478, nearly seven years afterwards.

22 To *abase* is to *cast down*, to *lower*, or to *let fall.*

23 A small coin, the twelfth part of a French *sous.*

24 *Marvellous* is here used adverbially. *Proper* for *handsome* or *well-
proportioned.* See *The Merchant*, page 91, note 17.

25 Shakespeare uses *in* or *into* indifferently, as suits his verse.

SCENE III. — *The Same.   A Room in the Palace.*

Enter Queen ELIZABETH, RIVERS, *and* GREY.

Riv. Have patience, madam : there's no doubt his Majesty
Will soon recover his accustom'd health.

Grey. In that you brook it ill, it makes him worse :
Therefore, for God's sake, entertain good comfort,
And cheer his Grace with quick [1] and merry words.

Q. Eliz. If he were dead, what would betide of me?

Riv. No other harm but loss of such a lord.

Q. Eliz. The loss of such a lord includes all harms.

Grey. The Heavens have bless'd you with a goodly son,
To be your comforter when he is gone.

Q. Eliz. Ah, he is young ; and his minority
Is put into the trust of Richard Gloster,
A man that loves not me nor none of you.

Riv. Is it concluded he shall be protector?

Q. Eliz. It is determined, not concluded [2] yet :
But so it must be, if the King miscarry.

Enter BUCKINGHAM *and* STANLEY.[3]

Grey. Here come the Lords of Buckingham and Stanley.

---

[1] *Quick*, here, is *lively, sprightly.* So in *Love's Labours Lost*, i. 1 : "But
is there no *quick* recreation granted ? "

[2] A thing was said to be *determined*, when it was *resolved* upon ; *concluded*, when it was *formally passed*, so as to be a ground of action.

[3] Henry Stafford, the present Duke of Buckingham, was descended, on
his father's side, from Thomas of Woodstock, the fifth son of Edward III.
On his mother's side he was descended from John of Ghent, third son of
the same great Edward. He was as accomplished and as unprincipled as
he was nobly descended. — Thomas Lord Stanley was Lord Steward of the
King's household to Edward IV.

Buck. Good time of day unto your royal Grace !

Stan. God make your Majesty joyful as you have been !

Q. Eliz. The Countess Richmond,[4] good my Lord of
      Stanley,
To your good prayer will scarcely say amen.
Yet, Stanley, notwithstanding she's your wife,
And loves not me, be you, good lord, assured
I hate not you for her proud arrogance.

Stan. I do beseech you, either not believe
The envious slanders of her false accusers ;
Or, if she be accused on true report,
Bear with her weakness, which, I think, proceeds
From wayward sickness, and no grounded malice.

Riv. Saw you the King to-day, my Lord of Stanley ?

Stan. But now the Duke of Buckingham and I
Are come from visiting his Majesty.

Q. Eliz. What likelihood of his amendment, lords ?

Buck. Madam, good hope ; his Grace speaks cheerfully.

Q. Eliz. God grant him health ! Did you confer with
      him ?

Buck. Ay, madam : he desires to make atonement [5]
Between the Duke of Gloster and your brothers,
And between them and my Lord Chamberlain ;

---

[4] The Countess of Richmond was Margaret, the only child of John Beaufort, the first Duke of Somerset, and so was descended from John of Ghent
through the Beaufort branch of his family ; born out of wedlock. Margaret's
first husband was Edmund, Earl of Richmond, son of Owen Tudor, by
whom she became the mother of Henry VII. Afterwards she was married
successively to Sir Henry Stafford, uncle of Buckingham, and to the Lord
Stanley of this play, but had no more children. She lived to a great age,
and was so highly reputed for prudence and virtue, that her grandson,
Henry VIII., was mainly guided by her advice in forming his first council.

[5] *Atonement* is *reconciliation, at-one-ment.* See *As You Like It*, page 137,
note 20.

And sent to warn [6] them to his royal presence.

    Q. Eliz. Would all were well! but that will never be:
I fear our happiness is at the height.

Enter GLOSTER, HASTINGS, *and* DORSET.

    Glos. They do me wrong, and I will not endure it:
Who are they that complain unto the King
That I, forsooth, am stern, and love them not?
By holy Paul, they love his Grace but lightly
That fill his ears with such dissentious rumours.
Because I cannot flatter and speak fair,
Smile in men's faces, smooth, deceive, and cog, [7]
Duck with French nods and apish courtesy,
I must be held a rancorous enemy.
Cannot a plain man live and think no harm,
But thus his simple truth must be abused
By silken, sly, insinuating Jacks?

    Riv. To whom in all this presence speaks your Grace?

    Glos. To thee, that hast nor honesty nor grace.
When have I injured thee? when done thee wrong?—
Or thee?—or thee?—or any of your faction?
A plague upon you all! His royal Grace—
Whom God preserve better than you would wish!—
Cannot be quiet scarce a breathing-while,
But you must trouble him with lewd [8] complaints.

    Q. Eliz. Brother of Gloster, you mistake the matter.
The King, of his own royal disposition,

---

    [6] To *warn* was used for to *summon.*

    [7] To *smooth,* or to *soothe,* is, in old language, to *insinuate* and *beguile* with flattery; to *cog,* is to *cajole* and *cheat.* Repeatedly so. See *Much Ado,* page 109, note 8.

    [8] *Lewd* in its old sense of *knavish, wicked,* or *base.*

And not provoked by any suitor else ;
Aiming, belike, at your interior hatred,
That in your outward action shows itself
Against my children, brothers, and myself,
Makes him to send, that thereby he may gather
The ground of your ill-will, and so remove it.

   Glos. I cannot tell : the world is grown so bad,
That wrens may prey where eagles dare not perch :
Since every Jack became a gentleman,
There's many a gentle person made a Jack.[9]

   Q. Eliz. Come, come, we know your meaning, brother
     Gloster ;
You envy my advancement and my friends' :
God grant we never may have need of you !

   Glos. Meantime, God grants that we have need of you :
Our brother is imprison'd by your means,
Myself disgraced, and the nobility
Held in contempt ; while great promotions
Are daily given to ennoble those
That scarce, some two days since, were worth a noble.

   Q. Eliz. By Him that raised me to this careful height
From that contented hap which I enjoy'd,
I never did incense his Majesty
Against the Duke of Clarence, but have been
An earnest advocate to plead for him.
My lord, you do me shameful injury,
Falsely to draw me in these vile suspects.

   Glos. You may deny that you were not the cause

---

[9] *Jack* was a common term of contempt or reproach. Richard is referring to the Queen's kindred, her sons, the Greys, and her brothers, the
Woodvilles, who, by her marriage with the King, were suddenly raised
from a far inferior rank to all but the highest.

Of my Lord Hastings' late imprisonment.

    Riv. She may, my lord; for —

    Glos. She may, Lord Rivers! why, who knows not so?
She may do more, sir, than denying that:
She may help you to many fair preferments;
And then deny her aiding hand therein,
And lay those honours on your high desert.
What may she not? She may, — ay, marry, may she, —

    Riv. What, marry, may she?

    Glos. What, marry, may she! marry with a king,
A bachelor, a handsome stripling too:
I wis [10] your grandam had a worser match.

    Q. Eliz. My Lord of Gloster, I have too long borne
Your blunt upbraidings and your bitter scoffs:
By Heaven, I will acquaint his Majesty
With those gross taunts I often have endured.
I had rather be a country servant-maid
Than a great queen, with this condition,
To be so baited, scorn'd, and stormèd at:

Enter Queen MARGARET, *behind.*

Small joy have I in being England's Queen.

    Q. Mar. [*Aside.*] And lessen'd be that small, God, I be-
    seech Him!
Thy honour, state, and seat is due to me.

    Glos. What! threat you me with telling of the King?
Tell him, and spare not: look, what I have said
I will avouch in presence of the King:

---

    10 Dyce thinks that the writers of Shakespeare's time used *I wis* "as
equivalent to *I ween.*" Here it seems to have about the sense of *I think,
I guess,* or, as they say at the South, *I reckon.* See *The Merchant,* page 130,
note 9.

I dare adventure to be sent to th' Tower.
'Tis time to speak; my pains are quite forgot.

 Q. Mar. [*Aside.*] Out, devil! I remember them too
  well:
Thou kill'dst my husband Henry in the Tower,
And Edward, my poor son, at Tewksbury.

 Glos. Ere you were queen, ay, or your husband king,
I was a pack-horse in his great affairs;
A weeder-out of his proud adversaries,
A liberal rewarder of his friends:
To royalize his blood I spilt mine own.

 Q. Mar. [*Aside.*] Ay, and much better blood than his
  or thine.

 Glos. In all which time you and your husband Grey
Were factious for the House of Lancaster;—
And, Rivers, so were you:—was not your husband
In Margaret's battle [11] at Saint Alban's slain?
Let me put in your minds, if you forget,
What you have been ere now, and what you are;
Withal, what I have been, and what I am.

 Q. Mar. [*Aside.*] A murderous villain, and so still thou
  art.

[11] *Battle* here probably means *army.* A common use of the word in old
writers.—Sir John Grey, the Queen's former husband, fell in what is known
as the second battle of Saint Alban's, which took place February 18, 1461.
In that battle the Lancastrians were victorious, Queen Margaret being at
the head of the army on that side. Their advantage, however, was much
more than lost at the great battle of Towton, fought on the 29th of March
following, and one of the fiercest and bloodiest in the long series of wars
known as the Wars of the Roses. Upon this triumph of the Yorkists, many
of the Lancastrians, and among them the Greys, were attainted, and stripped
of their possessions. It was upon her throwing herself at the feet of King
Edward, and soliciting a reversal of the attainder in behalf of her destitute
children, that the Lady Grey first won his pity, which soon warmed into
love. See Third Part of *Henry the Sixth*, iii. 2.

  Glos. Poor Clarence did forsake his father, Warwick;
Ay, and forswore himself,—which Jesu pardon!—

  Q. Mar. [*Aside.*] Which God revenge!

  Glos. —To fight on Edward's party, for the crown;
And for his meed, poor lord, he is mew'd up.
I would to God my heart were flint, like Edward's;
Or Edward's soft and pitiful, like mine:
I am too childish-foolish for this world.

  Q. Mar. [*Aside.*] Hie thee to Hell for shame, and
      leave this world,
Thou cacodemon![12] there thy kingdom is.

  Riv. My Lord of Gloster, in those busy days
Which here you urge to prove us enemies,
We follow'd then our lord, our lawful King:
So should we you, if you should be our king.

  Glos. If I should be! I had rather be a pedler:
Far be it from my heart, the thought of it!

  Q. Eliz. As little joy, my lord, as you suppose
You should enjoy, were you this country's King,
As little joy may you suppose in me,
That I enjoy, being the Queen thereof.

  Q. Mar. [*Aside.*] As little joy enjoys the Queen thereof;
For I am she, and altogether joyless.
I can no longer hold me patient. —   [*Advancing.*
Hear me, you wrangling pirates, that fall out
In sharing that which you have pill'd[13] from me!
Which of you trembles not that looks on me?
If not, that, I being queen, you bow like subjects,
Yet that, by you deposed, you quake like rebels?—

---

[12] A *cacodemon* is an evil spirit, a fiend. The word is Greek.

[13] To *pill* is to *pillage*. It is often used with to *poll* or *strip*. "Kildare did use to *pill and poll* his friendes, tenants, and reteyners." — HOLINSHED.

Ah, gentle villain, do not turn away !

Glos. Foul wrinkled witch, what makest[14] thou in my
    sight?

Q. Mar. But repetition of what thou hast marr'd ;
That will I make before I let thee go.

Glos. Wert thou not banishéd on pain of death?[15]

Q. Mar. I was ;
But I do find more pain in banishment
Than death can yield me here by my abode.
A husband and a son thou owest to me, —
And thou a kingdom, — all of you allegiance :
The sorrow that I have, by right is yours ;
And all the pleasures you usurp are mine.

Glos. The curse my noble father laid on thee,
When thou didst crown his warlike brows with paper,
And with thy scorns drew'st rivers from his eyes ;
And then, to dry them, gavest the duke a clout
Steep'd in the faultless blood of pretty Rutland ; —
His curses, then from bitterness of soul
Denounced against thee, are all fall'n upon thee ;
And God, not we, hath plagued thy bloody deed.[16]

Q. Eliz. So just is God, to right the innocent.

---

[14] " What *makest* thou " is old language for "what *doest* thou." Here it
means, "what business have you in this place?" See *As You Like It*,
page 57, note 4. — *Gentle*, in the line before, is *high-born*.

[15] Margaret fled into France after the battle of Hexham, in 1464, and
Edward issued a proclamation prohibiting any of his subjects from aiding
her return, or harbouring her, should she attempt to revisit England. She
remained abroad till April, 1471, when she landed at Weymouth. After
the battle of Tewksbury, in May, 1471, she was confined in the Tower,
where she continued a prisoner till 1475, when she was ransomed by her
father Reignier, and removed to France, where she died in 1482.

[16] The matter here referred to is set forth at length in the Third Part of
Henry the Sixth, Act i. scene 4.

Hast. O, 'twas the foulest deed to slay that babe,
And the most merciless that e'er was heard of !

Riv. Tyrants themselves wept when it was reported.

Dor. No man but prophesied revenge for it.

Buck. Northumberland, then present, wept to see it.

Q. Mar. What ! were you snarling all before I came,
Ready to catch each other by the throat,
And turn you all your hatred now on me?
Did York's dread curse prevail so much with Heaven,
That Henry's death, my lovely Edward's death,
Their kingdom's loss, my woeful banishment,
Could all but answer for that peevish brat?
Can curses pierce the clouds and enter Heaven? —
Why, then give way, dull clouds, to my quick curses ! —
Though not by war, by surfeit die your King,
As ours by murder, to make him a king !
Edward thy son, that now is Prince of Wales,
For Edward my son, that was Prince of Wales,
Die in his youth by like untimely violence !
Thyself a queen, for me that was a queen,
Outlive thy glory, like my wretched self !
Long mayst thou live to wail thy children's loss ;
And see another, as I see thee now,
Deck'd in thy rights, as thou art stall'd in mine !
Long die thy happy days before thy death ;
And, after many lengthen'd hours of grief,
Die neither mother, wife, nor England's Queen ! —
Rivers and Dorset, you were standers-by, —
And so wast thou, Lord Hastings, — when my son
Was stabb'd with bloody daggers : God, I pray Him,
That none of you may live his natural age,
But by some unlook'd accident cut off !

Glos. Have done thy charm, thou hateful wither'd
    hag !

Q. Mar. And leave out thee? stay, dog, for thou shalt
    hear me.

If Heaven have any grievous plague in store
Exceeding those that I can wish upon thee,
O, let them [17] keep it till thy sins be ripe,
And then hurl down their indignation
On thee, the troubler of the poor world's peace !
The worm of conscience still be-gnaw thy soul !
Thy friends suspect for traitors while thou livest,
And take deep traitors for thy dearest friends !
No sleep close up that deadly eye of thine,
Unless it be while some tormenting dream
Affrights thee with a hell of ugly devils !
Thou elvish-mark'd, abortive, rooting hog ! [18]
Thou that wast seal'd in thy nativity
The slave of Nature and the son of Hell !
Thou slander of thy heavy mother's womb !
Thou loathèd issue of thy father's loins !
Thou rag of honour ! thou detested —

    Glos. Margaret.

    Q. Mar.   Richard !

    Glos.   Ha !

    Q. Mar.   I call thee not.

    Glos. I cry thee mercy, then ; for I did think

---

[17] *Them* refers to *Heaven*, the latter being a collective noun.

[18] She calls him *hog*, in allusion to his cognizance, which was a *boar*.
"The expression," says Warburton, "is fine: remembering her youngest
son, she alludes to the ravage which hogs make with the finest flowers in
gardens; and intimating that Elizabeth was to expect no other treatment
for her sons." — *Elvish-mark'd* refers to the old belief that deformities of
person were the work of malignant or mischievous fairies or *elves*.

That thou hadst call'd me all these bitter names.

    Q. Mar. Why, so I did; but look'd for no reply.
O, let me make the period to my curse!

    Glos. 'Tis done by me, and ends in — Margaret.

    Q. Eliz. Thus have you breathed your curse against your-
       self.

    Q. Mar. Poor painted Queen, vain flourish of my fortune!
Why strew'st thou sugar on that bottled spider,[19]
Whose deadly web ensnareth thee about?
Fool, fool! thou whett'st a knife to kill thyself.
The day will come that thou shalt wish for me
To help thee curse that poisonous bunch-back'd toad.

    Hast. False-boding woman, end thy frantic curse,
Lest to thy harm thou move our patience.

    Q. Mar. Foul shame upon you! you have all moved mine.

    Riv. Were you well served, you would be taught your duty.

    Q. Mar. To serve me well, you all should do me duty,
Teach me to be your queen, and you my subjects:
O, serve me well, and teach yourselves that duty!

    Dor. Dispute not with her; she is lunatic.

    Q. Mar. Peace, master marquess, you are malapert:
Your fire-new[20] stamp of honour is scarce current:
O, that your young nobility could judge
What 'twere to lose it, and be miserable!
They that stand high have many blasts to shake them;
And if they fall, they dash themselves to pieces.

    Glos. Good counsel, marry: — learn it, learn it, marquess.

    Dor. It touches you, my lord, as much as me.

    Glos. Ay, and much more; but I was born so high:

----

[19] Alluding to Richard's form and venom. A *bottled spider* is a *large,
bloated spider;* supposed to contain venom in proportion to its size.

[20] *Fire-new* is the old term for what we call *brand-new.*

Our eyrie [21] buildeth in the cedar's top,
And dallies with the wind, and scorns the Sun.

Q. Mar. And turns the Sun to shade ; — alas ! alas ! —
Witness my son, now in the shade of death ;
Whose bright out-shining beams thy cloudy wrath
Hath in eternal darkness folded up.
Your eyrie buildeth in our eyrie's nest : —
O God, that see'st it, do not suffer it ;
As it was won with blood, lost be it so !

Riv. Peace, peace, for shame, if not for charity.

Q. Mar. Urge neither charity nor shame to me :
Uncharitably with me have you dealt,
And shamefully by you my hopes are butcher'd.
My charity is outrage, life my shame ; [22]
And in that shame still live my sorrow's rage !

Buck. Have done, have done.

Q. Mar. O princely Buckingham, I'll kiss thy hand,
In sign of league and amity with thee :
Now fair befall thee and thy noble House !
Thy garments are not spotted with our blood,
Nor thou within the compass of my curse.

Buck. Nor no one here ; for curses never pass
The lips of those that breathe them in the air.

Q. Mar. I'll not believe but they ascend the sky,
And there awake God's gentle-sleeping peace.
O Buckingham, take heed of yonder dog !

---

[21] *Eyrie* for *brood*. This word properly signified a brood of eagles, or hawks ; though in later times often used for the nest of those birds of prey. Its etymology is from *eyren*, eggs.

[22] "Outrage is the only charity shown me, and a life of shame, dishonour, is all the life permitted me." "*My* charity" may mean either the charity done *by* me or that done *to* me ; here it means the latter. For similar instances of construction, see *The Tempest*, page 138, note 23.

Look, when he fawns he bites ; and, when he bites,
His venom tooth will rankle to the death :
Have not to do with him, beware of him ;
Sin, death, and Hell have set their marks on him ;
And all their ministers attend on him.

 Glos. What doth she say, my Lord of Buckingham?

 Buck. Nothing that I respect, my gracious lord.

 Q. Mar. What, dost thou scorn me for my gentle counsel?
And soothe the devil that I warn thee from?
O, but remember this another day,
When he shall split thy very heart with sorrow,
And say, poor Margaret was a prophetess !—
Live each of you the subjects to his hate,
And he to yours, and all of you to God's ! *[Exit.*

 Hast. My hair doth stand on end to hear her curses.

 Riv. And so doth mine : I muse [23] why she's at liberty.

 Glos. I cannot blame her : by God's holy Mother,
She hath had too much wrong ; and I repent
My part thereof that I have done to her.

 Q. Eliz. I never did her any, to my knowledge.

 Glos. Yet you have all the vantage of her wrong.
I was too hot to do somebody good
That is too cold in thinking of it now.
Marry, as for Clarence, he is well repaid ;
He is frank'd up [24] to fatting for his pains :
God pardon them that are the cause of it !

 Riv. A virtuous and a Christian-like conclusion,
To pray for them that have done scathe to us.

---

[23] To *muse* is, in old usage, to *marvel* or to *wonder.*

[24] A *frank* is a *pen* or *coop* in which hogs and other animals were confined while fatting. To be *franked up* was to be *closely confined.* To
franch, or *frank,* was to stuff, to cram, or fatten.

Glos. So do I ever, being well advised ; [25] —
[*Aside.*] For, had I cursed now, I had cursed myself.

Enter CATESBY.

Cates. Madam, his Majesty doth call for you, —
And for your Grace, — and you, my noble lords.
    Q. Eliz. Catesby, I come. — Lords, will you go with me ?
    Riv. We wait upon your Grace.
                            [*Exeunt all but* GLOSTER.
    Glos. I do the wrong, and first begin to brawl.
The secret mischiefs that I set abroach
I lay unto the grievous charge of others.
Clarence, whom I indeed have laid in darkness,
I do beweep to many simple gulls ;
Namely, to Hastings, Stanley, Buckingham ;
And say it is the Queen and her allies
That stir the King against the duke my brother.
Now, they believe it ; and withal whet me
To be revenged on Rivers, Vaughan, Grey :
But then I sigh ; and, with a piece of Scripture,
Tell them that God bids us do good for evil :
And thus I clothe my naked villainy
With old odd ends stol'n out of Holy Writ ;
And seem a saint, when most I play the devil.
But, soft ! here come my executioners. —

Enter *two* Murderers.

How now, my hardy, stout-resolvèd [26] mates !

---

[25] " Being well advised " is the same as having well considered, or, as we now say, speaking or acting advisedly.   See *The Merchant*, page 180, note 1. — *Scathe*, in the line before, is an old word for *harm*.

[26] *Stout-resolved* is the same in sense as *boldly resolute ;* or, as we might say, men of iron resolution.

Are you now going to dispatch this thing?

1 Murd. We are, my lord; and come to have the
  warrant,
That we may be admitted where he is.

Glos. Well thought upon; I have it here about me:

  [*Gives the warrant.*

When you have done, repair to Crosby-place.
But, sirs, be sudden in the execution,
Withal obdúrate, do not hear him plead;
For Clarence is well-spoken, and perhaps
May move your hearts to pity, if you mark him.

1 Murd. Tut, tut, my lord, we will not stand to prate;
Talkers are no good doers: be assured
We go to use our hands, and not our tongues.

Glos. Your eyes drop millstones,[27] when fools' eyes drop
  tears:
I like you, lads; about your business straight;
Go, go, dispatch.

1 Murd.   We will, my noble lord.   [*Exeunt.*

SCENE IV. — *The Same.   A Room in the Tower.*

Enter CLARENCE *and* BRAKENBURY.

Brak. Why looks your Grace so heavily to-day?

Clar. O, I have pass'd a miserable night,
So full of fearful dreams, of ugly sights,
That, as I am a Christian faithful man,
I would not spend another such a night,

---

[27] *Weeping mill-stones* was a proverbial phrase used of persons not apt
to weep.   It occurs in the tragedy of *Cæsar and Pompey*, 1607.   "Men's eyes
must mill-stones drop. when fools shed tears."

Though 'twere to buy a world of happy days;
So full of dismal terror was the time!

    Brak. What was your dream, my lord? I pray you, tell me.

    Clar. Methought that I had broken from the Tower,
And was embark'd to cross to Burgundy; [1]
And, in my company, my brother Gloster;
Who from my cabin tempted me to walk
Upon the hatches: thence we look'd toward England,
And cited up a thousand heavy times,
During the wars of York and Lancaster,
That had befall'n us.   As we paced along
Upon the giddy footing of the hatches,
Methought that Gloster stumbled; and, in falling,
Struck me, that thought to stay him, overboard
Into the tumbling billows of the main.
O Lord! methought, what pain it was to drown!
What dreadful noise of water in mine ears!
What ugly sights of death within mine eyes!
Methought I saw a thousand fearful wrecks;
A thousand men that fishes gnaw'd upon;
Wedges of gold, great anchors, heaps of pearl,
Inestimable stones, unvalued [2] jewels,
All scattered in the bottom of the sea:
Some lay in dead men's skulls; and, in those holes
Where eyes did once inhabit, there were crept —
As 'twere in scorn of eyes — reflecting gems,
That woo'd the slimy bottom of the deep,
And mock'd the dead bones that lay scatter'd by.

---

[1] Clarence was desirous to aid his sister Margaret against the French King, who invaded her jointure lands after the death of her husband, Charles Duke of Burgundy, who was killed at Nanci, in January, 1477.

[2] *Unvalued* for *invaluable*, not to be valued, inestimable.

   Brak. Had you such leisure in the time of death
To gaze upon the secrets of the deep?
   Clar. Methought I had; and often did I strive
To yield the ghost: but still the envious [3] flood
Stopt-in my soul, and would not let it forth
To find the empty, vast, and wandering air;
But smother'd it within my panting bulk,[4]
Which almost burst to belch it in the sea.
   Brak. Awaked you not with this sore agony?
   Clar. No, no, my dream was lengthen'd after life:
O, then began the tempest to my soul!
I pass'd, methought, the melancholy flood,
With that grim ferryman which poets write of,
Unto the kingdom of perpetual night.
The first that there did greet my stranger soul
Was my great father-in-law, renownèd Warwick;
Who cried aloud, *What scourge for perjury*
Can this dark monarchy afford false Clarence?
And so he vanish'd: then came wandering by
A shadow like an angel, with bright hair
Dabbled in blood; and he shriek'd out aloud,

---

   [3] *Envious* in the sense of *malicious*, which was then its more common meaning. So in the preceding scene: "The *envious* slanders of her false accusers."

   [4] *Bulk* was used for *breast*. So in *Hamlet*, ii. 2: "He raised a sigh so piteous and profound, that it did seem to shatter all his *bulk*, and end his being." — *Vast*, in the line before, is *void* or *waste;* like the Latin *vastus.* — The "wandering air" is the aerial expanse where the soul would be free to use its wings, and roam at large. So in the description of Raphael's voyage to the Earth, *Paradise Lost*, v. 267:

> He speeds, and through the vast ethereal sky
> Sails between worlds and worlds, with steady wing,
> Now on the polar winds, then with quick fan
> Winnows the buxom air.

Clarence is come, false, fleeting,[5] *perjured Clarence,*
That stabb'd me in the field by Tewksbury:
Seize on him, Furies, take him to your torments!
With that, methought, a legion of foul fiends
Environ'd me, and howlèd in mine ears
Such hideous cries, that, with the very noise,
I trembling waked, and, for a season after,
Could not believe but that I was in Hell;
Such terrible impression made my dream.

Brak. No marvel, lord, though it affrighted you;
I am afraid, methinks, to hear you tell it.

Clar. O Brakenbury, I have done those things,
That now give evidence against my soul,
For Edward's sake; and see how he requites me!—
O God! if my deep prayers cannot appease Thee,
But Thou wilt be avengèd on my misdeeds,
Yet execute Thy will on me alone;
O, spare my guiltless wife[6] and my poor children!—
Keeper, I pr'ythee, sit by me awhile;
My soul is heavy, and I fain would sleep.

Brak. I will, my lord: God give your Grace good rest!—
                    [CLARENCE *sleeps in a chair.*
Sorrow breaks seasons and reposing hours,
Makes the night morning, and the noontide night.
Princes have but their titles for their glories,
An outward honour for an inward toil;
And, for unfelt imaginations,

---

[5] *Fleeting* or *flitting*, in old language, was used for *uncertain, inconstant, fluctuating.* Clarence broke his oath with the Earl of Warwick, and joined the army of his brother Edward.

[6] The wife of Clarence died before he was apprehended and confined in the Tower. See page 52, note 23.

They often feel a world of restless cares : [7]
So that, between their titles and low name,
There's nothing differs but the outward fame.

Enter the two Murderers.

1 Murd. Ho ! who's here?

Brak. What wouldst thou, fellow? and how camest thou
     hither?

1 Murd. I would speak with Clarence, and I came hither
on my legs.

Brak. What, so brief?

2 Murd. 'Tis better, sir, than to be tedious. — Let him
see our commission ; and talk no more.

          [*1* Murd. *gives a paper to* BRAK., *who reads it.*

Brak. I am, in this, commanded to deliver
The noble Duke of Clarence to your hands :
I will not reason what is meant hereby,
Because I will be guiltless of the meaning.
Here are the keys ; there sits the duke asleep :
I'll to the King ; and signify to him
That thus I have resign'd to you my charge.

1 Murd. You may, sir ; 'tis a point of wisdom : fare you
well.   [*Exit* BRAKENBURY.

2 Murd. What, shall we stab him as he sleeps?

1 Murd. No ; he'll say 'twas done cowardly, when he
wakes.

2 Murd. When he wakes ! why, fool, he shall never wake
till the judgment-day.

1 Murd. Why, then he'll say we stabb'd him sleeping.

---

[7] For imaginary pleasures which are unfelt by them, they often endure a
great burden of restless cares, which they feel, to their cost.

2 Murd. The urging of that word *judgment* hath bred a kind of remorse in me.

1 Murd. What, art thou afraid?

2 Murd. Not to kill him, having a warrant for it; but to be damn'd for killing him, from the which no warrant can defend me.

1 Murd. I thought thou hadst been resolute.

2 Murd. So I am, to let him live.

1 Murd. I'll back to the Duke of Gloster, and tell him so.

2 Murd. Nay, I pr'ythee, stay a little: I hope my holy humour will change; it was wont to hold me but while one tells twenty.

1 Murd. How dost thou feel thyself now?

2 Murd. Faith, some certain dregs of conscience are yet within me.

1 Murd. Remember our reward, when the deed's done.

2 Murd. Zounds, he dies: I had forgot the reward.

1 Murd. Where's thy conscience now?

2 Murd. In the Duke of Gloster's purse.

1 Murd. So, when he opens his purse to give us our reward, thy conscience flies out.

2 Murd. 'Tis no matter; let it go; there's few or none will entertain it.

1 Murd. What if it come to thee again?

2 Murd. I'll not meddle with it; it makes a man a coward: a man cannot steal, but it accuseth him; a man cannot swear, but it checks him: 'tis a blushing shame-faced spirit that mutinies in a man's bosom; it fills one full of obstacles: it made me once restore a purse of gold, that by chance I found; it beggars any man that keeps it: it is turn'd out of all towns and cities for a dangerous thing; and every man that means to live well endeavours to trust to himself and live without it.

1 Murd. Zounds, it is even now at my elbow, persuading me not to kill the duke.

2 Murd. Take the Devil in thy mind, and believe him not :[8] he would insinuate with thee but to make thee sigh.

1 Murd. I am strong-framed ; he cannot prevail with me.

2 Murd. Spoke like a tall fellow[9] that respects his reputation. Come, shall we fall to work?

1 Murd. Take him over the costard with the hilts[10] of thy sword, and then throw him into the malmsey-butt in the next room.

2 Murd. O excellent device ! and make a sop[11] of him.

1 Murd. Soft ! he wakes.

2 Murd. Strike !

1 Murd. No, we'll reason[12] with him.

---

[8] *Him* refers to *conscience*, not to *Devil.* — To *insinuate with* is to *make friends with*, to *play upon*, to *beguile*. The idea of conscience trying to wheedle and steal a man out of the Devil's leading is a most Shakesperian stroke of art. And the grim humour of these hired cut-throats in thus jesting away the approaches of preventive remorse is a capital instance of the Poet's inwardness with Nature. For even so men often laugh and sport themselves through the perpetration of crime; the supremacy of the moral law, the self-assertive rights of conscience instinctively prompting them to such tricks of evasion. I can hardly think of any one particular wherein Shakespeare's moral sanity of genius is more pregnantly manifested.

[9] That is, a *bold, stout-hearted* fellow. See *Twelfth Night*, page 35, note 4.

[10] *Hilts*, the plural form, was commonly used where we should use *hilt*. — *Costard*, of course, is put for *head*. The word properly means *apple*, and was thus applied from similarity of shape.

[11] A *sop* is anything soaked or steeped in liquor.

[12] Here, as often, to *reason* is to *talk* or *converse*. See *The Merchant*, page 126, note 3. — *Soft !* second line before, is the old exclamative for *hold ! stay !* or *not too fast !*

Clar. [*Waking.*] Where art thou, keeper? give me a cup
of wine.

1 Murd. You shall have wine enough, my lord, anon.

Clar. In God's name, what art thou?

1 Murd. A man, as you are.

Clar. But not, as I am, royal.

1 Murd. Nor you, as we are, loyal.

Clar. Thy voice is thunder, but thy looks are humble.

1 Murd. My voice is now the King's, my looks mine
own.

Clar. How darkly and how deadly dost thou speak!
Your eyes do menace me: why look you pale?
Who sent you hither? Wherefore do you come?

Both Murd. To, to, to —

Clar. To murder me?

Both Murd. Ay, ay.

Clar. You scarcely have the hearts to tell me so,
And therefore cannot have the hearts to do it.
Wherein, my friends, have I offended you?

1 Murd. Offended us you have not, but the King.

Clar. I shall be reconciled to him again.

2 Murd. Never, my lord; therefore prepare to die.

Clar. Are you call'd forth from out a world of men
To slay the innocent? What is my offence?
Where is the evidence that doth accuse me?
What lawful quest [13] have given their verdict up
Unto the frowning judge? or who pronounced
The bitter sentence of poor Clarence' death?
Before I be convict [14] by course of law,

---

[13] *Quest* here means a *jury of inquest.*

[14] *Convict* for *convicted.* Such shortened preterites are very frequent.
See *The Tempest*, page 56, note 43.

To threaten me with death is most unlawful.
I charge you, as you hope to have redemption
By Christ's dear blood shed for our grievous sins,
That you depart, and lay no hands on me :
The deed you undertake is damnable.

   1 Murd. What we will do, we do upon command.

   2 Murd. And he that hath commanded is our King.

   Clar. Erroneous vassals ! the great King of kings
Hath in the table of His law commanded
That thou shalt do no murder : will you, then,
Spurn at His edict, and fulfil a man's ?
Take heed ; for He holds vengeance in His hand,
To hurl upon their heads that break His law.

   2 Murd. And that same vengeance doth He hurl on thee,
For false forswearing, and for murder too :
Thou didst receive the Sacrament to fight
In quarrel of the House of Lancaster.

   1 Murd. And, like a traitor to the name of God,
Didst break that vow ; and with thy treacherous blade
Unripp'dst the bowels of thy sovereign's son.

   2 Murd. Whom thou wast sworn to cherish and defend.

   1 Murd. How canst thou urge God's dreadful law to us,
When thou hast broke it in such dear degree ?

   Clar. Alas ! for whose sake did I that ill deed ?
For Edward, for my brother, for his sake :
He sends you not to murder me for this ;
For in that sin he is as deep as I.
If God will be avengèd for the deed,
O, know you yet, He doth it publicly :
Take not the quarrel from His powerful arm ;
He needs no indirect nor lawless course
To cut off those that have offended Him.

1 Murd. Who made thee, then, a bloody minister,
When gallant-springing brave Plantagenet,
That princely novice, was struck dead by thee?

Clar. My brother's love, the Devil, and my rage.

1 Murd. Thy brother's love, our duty, and thy fault,
Provoke us hither now to slaughter thee.

Clar. If you do love my brother, hate not me ;
I am his brother, and I love him well.
If you are hired for meed, go back again,
And I will send you to my brother Gloster,
Who shall reward you better for my life
Than Edward will for tidings of my death.

2 Murd. You are deceived, your brother Gloster hates
  you.

Clar. O, no, he loves me, and he holds me dear :
Go you to him from me.

Both Murd.   Ay, so we will.

Clar. Tell him, when that our princely father York
Bless'd his three sons with his victorious arm,
And charged us from his soul to love each other,
He little thought of this divided friendship :
Bid Gloster think of this, and he will weep.

1 Murd. Ay, millstones ; as he lesson'd us to weep.

Clar. O, do not slander him, for he is kind.

1 Murd. Right,
As snow in harvest.   Come, you deceive yourself :
'Tis he that sends us to destroy you here.

Clar. It cannot be ; for he bewept my fortune,
And hugg'd me in his arms, and swore, with sobs,
That he would labour my delivery.

1 Murd. Why, so he doth, when he delivers you
From this Earth's thraldom to the joys of Heaven.

2 Murd. Make peace with God, for you must die, my lord.

Clar. Hast thou that holy feeling in thy soul,
To counsel me to make my peace with God,
And art thou yet to thy own soul so blind,
That thou wilt war with God by murdering me?
Ah, sirs, consider, he that set you on
To do this deed will hate you for the deed.

2 Murd. What shall we do?

Clar.   Relent, and save your souls.

1 Murd. Relent! 'tis cowardly and womanish.

Clar. Not to relent is beastly, savage, devilish.
My friend, I spy some pity in thy looks:
O, if thine eye be not a flatterer,
Come thou on my side, and entreat for me:
A begging prince what beggar pities not?

1 Murd. Ay, [*Stabbing him.*] thus, and thus: if all this
        will not do,
I'll drown you in the malmsey-butt within.

                              [*Exit, with the body.*

2 Murd. A bloody deed, and desperately dispatch'd!
How fain, like Pilate, would I wash my hands
Of this most grievous murder!

Re-enter 1 Murderer.

1 Murd. How now! what mean'st thou, that thou help'st
        me not?
By Heaven, the duke shall know how slack you've been.

2 Murd. I would he knew that I had saved his brother!
Take thou the fee, and tell him what I say;
For I repent me that the duke is slain.   [*Exit.*

1 Murd. So do not I: go, coward as thou art. —
Well, I'll go hide the body in some hole,

Till that the duke give order for his burial :
And, when I have my meed, I will away ;
For this will out, and then I must not stay.[15]   [*Exit.*

ACT II.

Scene I.—*London.   A Room in the Palace.*

Enter King Edward, *led in sick,* Queen Elizabeth, Dorset, Rivers, Hastings, Buckingham, Grey, *and others.*

K. Edw. Why, so ; now have I done a good day's work :
You peers, continue this united league :
I every day expect an embassage
From my Redeemer to redeem me hence ;
And now in peace my soul shall part[1] to Heaven,
Since I have made my friends at peace on Earth.
Rivers and Hastings, take each other's hand ;
Dissemble not your hatred, swear your love.[2]

[15] The Duke of Clarence was arraigned for treason before the Parliament, convicted, and sentence of death passed upon him. This was in February, 1478, and a few days later it was announced that he had died in the Tower. So that this first Act of the play embraces a period of nearly seven years, the death of King Henry having occurred in May, 1471. The manner of Clarence's death has never been ascertained. It was generally attributed to the machinations of Richard. There was a fierce grudge between the two Dukes, growing out of their rapacity towards the Warwick estates. See page 52, note 24.

[1] *Part* for *depart ;* the two being often used indiscriminately.

[2] To *dissemble* is, strictly, to *put off* the show of what is, as to *simulate* is to *put on* the show of what is not. So here the meaning is, " Do not merely put off the show of hatred, but eradicate it altogether, and swear love into its place."

Riv. By Heaven, my soul is purged from grudging hate;
And with my hand I seal my true heart's love.

Hast. So thrive I, as I truly swear the like!

K. Edw. Take heed you dally not before your King;
Lest He that is the súpreme King of kings
Confound your hidden falsehood, and award
Either of you to be the other's end.

Hast. So prosper I, as I swear perfect love!

Riv. And I, as I love Hastings with my heart!

K. Edw. Madam, yourself are not exempt in this, —
Nor you, son Dorset, — Buckingham, nor you; —
You have been factious one against the other.
Wife, love Lord Hastings, let him kiss your hand;
And what you do, do it unfeignèdly.

Q. Eliz. There, Hastings; I will never more remember
Our former hatred, so thrive I and mine!

K. Edw. Dorset, embrace him; — Hastings, love lord
          marquess.

Dor. This interchange of love, I here protest,
Upon my part shall be inviolable.

Hast. And so swear I.   [*They embrace.*

K. Edw. Now, princely Buckingham, seal thou this league
With thy embracements to my wife's allies,
And make me happy in your unity.

Buck. [*To the* Queen.] Whenever Buckingham doth turn
          his hate
Upon your Grace, but[3] with all duteous love

---

[3] A very uncommon use of *but*, which is here equivalent to *and not*, or, better, to *or not*. The full sense appears to be, " Whenever Buckingham doth turn his hate upon you, *or rather* when he doth *not* with all duteous love," &c. For another like instance of *but*, see *The Winter's Tale*, page 69, note 19.

Doth cherish you and yours, God punish me
With hate in those where I expect most love !
When I have most need to employ a friend,
And most assurèd that he is a friend,
Deep, hollow, treacherous, and full of guile,
Be he unto me ! this do I beg of God,
When I am cold in zeal to you or yours.

[*Embracing* RIVERS, &c.

K. Edw. A pleasing cordial, princely Buckingham,
Is this thy vow unto my sickly heart.
There wanteth now our brother Gloster here,
To make the perfect period of this peace.

Buck. And, in good time, here comes the noble duke.

Enter GLOSTER.

Glos. Good morrow to my sovereign King and Queen ;
And, princely peers, a happy time of day !

K. Edw. Happy, indeed, as we have spent the day.
Brother, we have done deeds of charity ;
Made peace of enmity, fair love of hate,
Between these swelling wrong-incensèd peers.

Glos. A blessèd labour, my most sovereign liege.
Among this princely heap,[4] if any here,
By false intelligence or wrong surmise, hold me
A foe ; if I unwittingly, or in my rage,
Have aught committed that is hardly borne
By any in this presence, I desire
To reconcile me to his friendly peace :
'Tis death to me to be at enmity ;

---

4 *Heap* for *throng, crowd,* or *gathering,* occurs repeatedly. So in *Julius Cæsar,* i. 3 : " And there were drawn upon a *heap* a hundred ghastly women, transformèd with their fear."

I hate it, and desire all good men's love. —
First, madam, I entreat true peace of you,
Which I will purchase with my duteous service ; —
Of you, my noble cousin Buckingham,
If ever any grudge were lodged between us ; —
Of you, Lord Rivers, — and, Lord Grey, of you,
That all without desert have frown'd on me ; —
Dukes, earls, lords, gentlemen ; — indeed, of all.
I do not know that Englishman alive
With whom my soul is any jot at odds
More than the infant that is born to-night :
I thank my God for my humility.

   Q. Eliz. A holiday shall this be kept hereafter :
I would to God all strifes were well compounded. —
My sovereign lord, I do beseech your Highness
To take our brother Clarence to your grace.

  Glos. Why, madam, have I offer'd love for this,
To be so flouted in this royal presence ?
Who knows not that the gentle duke is dead ? [*They all start.*
You do him injury to scorn his corse.

   K. Edw. Who knows not he is dead ! who knows he is ?

   Q. Eliz. All-seeing Heaven, what a world is this !

   Buck. Look I so pale, Lord Dorset, as the rest ?

   Dor. Ay, my good lord ; and no one in this presence
But his red colour hath forsook his cheeks.

   K. Edw. Is Clarence dead ? the order was reversed.

   Glos. But he, poor man, by your first order died,
And that a wingèd Mercury did bear ;
Some tardy cripple bore the countermand,
That came too lag to see him buriéd.
God grant that some, less noble and less loyal,
Nearer in bloody thoughts, but not in blood,

Deserve not worse than wretched Clarence did,
And yet go current from suspicion !

Enter STANLEY.

Stan. A boon, my sovereign, for my service done !
K. Edw. I pr'ythee, peace ; my soul is full of sorrow.
Stan. I will not rise, unless your Highness hear me.
K. Edw. Then say at once what is it thou request'st.
Stan. The forfeit,[5] sovereign, of my servant's life ;
Who slew to-day a riotous gentleman
Lately attendant on the Duke of Norfolk.
K. Edw. Have I a tongue to doom my brother's death,
And shall that tongue give pardon to a slave?
My brother kill'd no man : his fault was thought,
And yet his punishment was bitter death.
Who sued to me for him? who, in my rage,
Kneel'd at my feet, and bade me be advised?[6]
Who spoke of brotherhood? who spoke of love?
Who told me how the poor soul did forsake
The mighty Warwick, and did fight for me?
Who told me, in the field at Tewksbury,
When Oxford had me down, he rescued me,
And said, *Dear brother, live, and be a king?*
Who told me, when we both lay in the field
Frozen almost to death, how he did lap me
Even in his garments, and did give himself,
All thin and naked, to the numb-cold night?
All this from my remembrance brutish wrath
Sinfully pluck'd, and not a man of you

---

5 He means a *remission* of the forfeit; the servant having *forfeited* his
life by the act of homicide.

6 *Advised*, again, for *considerate*, or *cautious*. See page 77, note 25.

Had so much grace to put it in my mind.
But when your carters or your waiting-vassals
Have done a drunken slaughter, and defaced
The precious image of our dear Redeemer,
You straight are on your knees for pardon, pardon;
And I, unjustly too, must grant it you:
But for my brother not a man would speak,
Nor I, ungracious, speak unto myself
For him, poor soul. The proudest of you all
Have been beholding [7] to him in his life;
Yet none of you would once plead for his life.—
O God, I fear Thy justice will take hold
On me, and you, and mine, and yours for this!—
Come, Hastings, help me to my closet.—Ah,
Poor Clarence!

[*Exeunt the* King, *the* Queen, HASTINGS, RIVERS,
DORSET, *and* GREY.

Glos. This is the fruit of rashness! Mark'd you not
How that the guilty kindred of the Queen
Look'd pale when they did hear of Clarence' death?
O, they did urge it still unto the King!
God will revenge it. But, come, let us in,
To comfort Edward with our company.

Buck. We wait upon your Grace. [*Exeunt.*

---

[7] *Beholding* where we should use *beholden.* Always so in Shakespeare.
The word means *obliged* or *indebted.*

SCENE II. — *The Same.   Another Room in the Palace.*

Enter the Duchess *of York,*[1] *with a* Son *and* Daughter *of* CLARENCE.

Son. Good grandam, tell us, is our father dead?

Duch. No, boy.

Daugh. Why do you weep so oft, and beat your breast,
And cry, *O Clarence, my unhappy son!*

Son. Why do you look on us, and shake your head,
And call us orphans, wretches, castaways,
If that our noble father be alive?

Duch. My pretty cousins,[2] you mistake me both;
I do lament the sickness of the King,
As loth to lose him, not your father's death:
It were lost sorrow to wail one that's lost.

Son. Then, grandam, you conclude that he is dead.
The King my uncle is to blame for this:
God will revenge it; whom I will impórtune
With daily prayers all to that effect.

Daugh. And so will I.

Duch. Peace, children, peace! the King doth love you well:
Incapable[3] and shallow innocents,

---

[1] Cicely, daughter of Ralph Neville, first Earl of Westmoreland, and widow of Richard Duke of York, who was killed at the battle of Wakefield, 1460. She survived her husband thirty-five years, living till the year 1495.

[2] The Duchess is speaking to her grandchildren, *cousin* being then used for this relation, as well as for *nephew*, *niece*, and indeed for *kindred* generally. The word *grandchild* does not occur in Shakespeare.

[3] *Incapable* is here used nearly, if not exactly, in the sense of *unconscious*; meaning that unconsciousness of evil which renders children *unsuspecting*. So in *Hamlet*, iv. 4: "As one *incapable* of her own distress."

You cannot guess who caused your father's death.

   Son. Grandam, we can; for my good uncle Gloster
Told me, the King, provoked to't by the Queen,
Devised impeachments to imprison him:
And, when my uncle told me so, he wept,
And pitied me, and kindly kiss'd my cheek;
Bade me rely on him as on my father,
And he would love me dearly as his child.

   Duch. Ah, that deceit should steal such gentle[4] shapes,
And with a virtuous visor hide deep vice!
He is my son; ay, and therein my shame;
Yet from my dugs[5] he drew not this deceit.

   Son. Think you my uncle did dissemble,[6] grandam?

   Duch. Ay, boy.

   Son. I cannot think it. Hark! what noise is this?

Enter Queen ELIZABETH, *distractedly;* RIVERS *and* DORSET
following her.

   Q. Eliz. O, who shall hinder me to wail and weep,
To chide my fortune, and torment myself?
I'll join with black despair against my soul,
And to myself become an enemy.

   Duch. What means this scene of rude impatience?[7]

   Q. Eliz. To make an act of tragic violence:

---

   [4] *Gentle* here means *well-born* or *high-born,* as opposed to *simple* or *low-born.* So in i. 3, of this play: "Ah, *gentle villain,* do not turn away." Spoken to Richard by Margaret.

   [5] This word was formerly thought good enough for the most refined lips and the choicest strains of poetry.

   [6] *Dissemble* was used, as it still is, both for *feigning* and for *concealing* thoughts and feelings. Here it has the sense of to *simulate* or to *feign.* See page 89, note 2.

   [7] The endings *-ience* and *-iance,* as well as *-ion, -ian,* and *-ious,* are often

Edward, my lord, thy son, our King, is dead !
Why grow the branches when the root is gone?
Why wither not the leaves that want their sap?
If you will live, lament ; if die, be brief,[8]
That our swift-wingèd souls may catch the King's ;
Or, like obedient subjects, follow him
To his new kingdom of perpetual rest.

 Duch. Ah, so much interest have I in thy sorrow
As I had title in thy noble husband !
I have bewept a worthy husband's death,
And lived by looking on his images :[9]
But now two mirrors of his princely semblance
Are crack'd in pieces by malignant death,
And I for comfort have but one false glass,
That grieves me when I see my shame in him.
Thou art a widow ; yet thou art a mother,
And hast the comfort of thy children left thee :
But death hath snatch'd my husband from mine arms,
And pluck'd two crutches from my feeble hands,
Clarence and Edward.   O, what cause have I—
Thine being but a moiety of my grief—
To over-go thy plaints and drown thy cries !

 Son. Ah, aunt, you wept not for our father's death !
How can we aid you with our kindred tears?

 Daugh. Our fatherless distress was left unmoan'd ;
Your widow-dolour likewise be unwept !

---

used as two syllables by Shakespeare, especially at the end of a verse. So,
here, *impatience* is, properly, four syllables. And so in the preceding scenes
we have the line, " Lest to thy harm thou move our *patience*," and the line,
" And, for unfelt imaginations " ; where *-ience* and *-ions* are strictly dissyllabic.

 [8] That is, " be *quick.*"   *Brief* is often used so, as also *briefly* for *quickly.*
So in *Macbeth*, ii. 1 : " Let's *briefly* put on manly readiness."

 [9] " His *images*" are the *children* who represented and resembled him.

Q. Eliz. Give me no help in lamentation ;
I am not barren to bring forth complaints :
All springs reduce [10] their currents to mine eyes,
That I, being govern'd by the watery Moon,
May send forth plenteous tears to drown the world !
Ah for my husband, for my dear lord Edward !
　Children. Ah for our father, for our dear lord Clarence !
　Duch. Alas for both, both mine, Edward and Clarence !
　Q. Eliz. What stay had I but Edward ? and he's gone.
　Children. What stay had we but Clarence ? and he's gone.
　Duch. What stays had I but they ? and they are gone.
　Q. Eliz. Was never widow had so dear a loss !
　Children. Were never orphans had so dear a loss !
　Duch. Was never mother had so dear a loss !
Alas, I am the mother of these griefs !
Their woes are parcell'd, mine are general.
She for an Edward weeps, and so do I ;
I for a Clarence weep, so doth not she :
These babes for Clarence weep, and so do I ;
I for an Edward weep, so do not they :—
Alas, you three, on me, threefold distress'd,
Pour all your tears ! I am your sorrow's nurse,
And I will pamper it with lamentations.
　Dor. Comfort, dear mother : God is much displeased
That you take with unthankfulness His doing :
In common worldly things 'tis call'd ungrateful
With dull unwillingness to repay a debt
Which with a bounteous hand was kindly lent ;
Much more to be thus opposite with Heaven,

---

[10] *Reduce* in the Latin sense of *lead* or *bring back*. Repeatedly so. In the next line, the Moon is called *watery* from her connection with the tides. In *Hamlet*, i. 1, she is called "the *moist* star," for the same reason.

For it requires the royal debt it lent you.

 Riv. Madam, bethink you, like a careful mother,
Of the young Prince your son : send straight for him ;
Let him be crown'd ; in him your comfort lives :
Drown desperate sorrow in dead Edward's grave,
And plant your joys in living Edward's throne.

Enter GLOSTER, BUCKINGHAM, STANLEY, HASTINGS, RATCLIFF,
    and others.

 Glos. Sister, have comfort : all of us have cause
To wail the dimming of our shining star ;
But none can cure their harms by wailing them. —
Madam, my mother, I do cry you mercy ; [11]
I did not see your Grace : humbly on my knee
I crave your blessing.

 Duch. God bless thee ; and put meekness in thy breast,
Love, charity, obedience, and true duty !

 Glos. Amen ; — [*Aside.*] and make me die a good old
   man !
That is the butt-end of a mother's blessing :
I marvel that her Grace did leave it out.

 Buck. You cloudy princes and heart-sorrowing peers,
That bear this mutual heavy load of moan,
Now cheer each other in each other's love :
Though we have spent our harvest of this King,
We are to reap the harvest of his son.
The broken rancour of your high-swoln hearts,
But lately splinter'd, knit, and join'd together,
Must gently be preserved, cherish'd, and kept : [12]

---

[11] " I cry you mercy " is an old phrase for " I ask your pardon."

[12] This passage is touched with a sort of grammatical paralysis, but the
sense is not very obscure. Their hearts had been swollen high with ran-

Me seemeth good, that, with some little train,
Forthwith from Ludlow the young Prince be fet [13]
Hither to London, to be crown'd our king.

 Riv. Why with some little train, my Lord of Buckingham?

 Buck. Marry, my lord, lest, by a multitude,
The new-heal'd wound of malice should break out;
Which would be so much the more dangerous,
By how much the Estate [14] is green and yet ungovern'd:
Where every horse bears his commanding rein,
And may direct his course as please himself,
As well the fear of harm as harm apparent,[15]
In my opinion, ought to be prevented.

 Glos. I hope the King made peace with all of us;
And the compáct is firm and true in me.

 Hast. And so in me; and so, I think, in all:
Yet, since it is but green, it should be put
To no apparent likelihood of breach,
Which haply by much company might be urged:
Therefore I say with noble Buckingham,
That it is meet so few should fetch the Prince.

 Stan. And so say I.

 Glos. Then be it so; and go we to determine
Who they shall be that straight shall post to Ludlow. —

cour, but the rancour has been broken out of them; and as the broken
parts have been but lately splintered, and knit and joined together, so the
union must be gently preserved, &c.

 13 *Fet* is an old preterite form of *fetch.* The poet has it in several other
instances. — Prince Edward, as Prince of Wales, was in fact living at this
time under the governance of his maternal uncle, the Earl of Rivers, at Ludlow Castle; his presence being deemed necessary to restrain the Welshmen,
who were something wild and apt to be disorderly.

 14 "The *Estate*" here means "the State." In reference to the governing
part of the Commonwealth, the two words anciently had the same meaning.

 15 *Apparent* in its old sense of *evident* or *manifest.* Repeatedly so.

Madam, — and you, my mother, — will you go
To give your censures [16] in this business?

                    [*Exeunt all but* BUCKINGHAM *and* GLOSTER.

  Buck. My lord, whoever journeys to the Prince,
For God's sake, let not us two stay at home;
For, by the way, I'll sort occasion,
As index [17] to the story we late talk'd of,
To part the Queen's proud kindred from the Prince.

  Glos. My other self, my counsel's consistory,
My oracle, my prophet! my dear cousin,
I, as a child, will go by thy direction.
Towards Ludlow then, for we'll not stay behind.   [*Exeunt.*

SCENE III. — *The Same.   A Street.*

Enter two Citizens, *meeting.*

  1 Cit. Good morrow, neighbour: whither away so fast?

  2 Cit. I promise you I scarcely know myself:
Hear you the news abroad?

  1 Cit.   Yes; that the King is dead.

  2 Cit. Ill news, by'r Lady; seldom comes the better:
I fear, I fear 'twill prove a giddy world.

Enter a third Citizen.

  3 Cit. Neighbours, God speed!

  1 Cit.   Give you good morrow, sir.

---

[16] That is, your *judgments*, your *opinions*. See *The Winter's Tale*, page 63, note 1.

[17] The *index* of a book was formerly set at the beginning; hence, probably, the word came to be used in the sense of *opening* or *introduction*. So in iv. 4 of this play: "The flattering *index* of a direful pageant." And in *Othello*, ii. 1: "An *index* and obscure *prologue* to the history of lust and foul thoughts." — *Sort*, in the line before, is used for *select* or *pick.*

3 Cit. Doth the news hold of good King Edward's death?

2 Cit. Ay, sir, it is too true ; God help, the while !

3 Cit. Then, masters, look to see a troublous world.

1 Cit. No, no ; by God's good grace his son shall reign.

3 Cit. Woe to that land that's govern'd by a child ![1]

2 Cit. In him there is a hope of government ;
That, in his nonage, Council under him,
And, in his full and ripen'd years, himself,
No doubt, shall then, and till then, govern well.[2]

1 Cit. So stood the State when Henry the Sixth
Was crown'd in Paris but at nine months old.

3 Cit. Stood the State so ? No, no, good friends, God wot ;
For then this land was famously enrich'd
With politic grave counsel ; then the King
Had virtuous uncles to protect his Grace.

1 Cit. Why, so hath this, both by his father and mother.

3 Cit. Better it were they all came by his father,
Or by his father there were none at all ;
For emulation now, who shall be nearest,
Will touch us all too near, if God prevent not.
O, full of danger is the Duke of Gloster !
And the Queen's sons and brothers haught and proud :
And, were they to be ruled, and not to rule,
This sickly land might solace as before.

1 Cit. Come, come, we fear the worst ; all will be well.

---

[1] So in *Ecclesiastes*, x. 16: "Woe to thee, O land ! when thy king is a child."

[2] We may hope well of his government in all circumstances ; we may hope this of his Council while he is in his nonage, and of himself in his riper years.

3 Cit. When clouds are seen, wise men put on their
        cloaks ;
When great leaves fall, then Winter is at hand ;
When the Sun sets, who doth not look for night?
Untimely storms make men expect a dearth.
All may be well ; but, if God sort [3] it so,
'Tis more than we deserve, or I expect.

2 Cit. Truly, the hearts of men are full of fear :
You cannot reason [4] almost with a man
That looks not heavily and full of dread.

3 Cit. Before the days of change, still [5] is it so :
By a divine instinct men's minds mistrust
Ensuing danger ; as, by proof, we see
The waters swell before a boisterous storm.
But leave it all to God.— Whither away?

2 Cit. Marry, we were sent for to the justices.

3 Cit. And so was I : I'll bear you company.   [*Exeunt.*

SCENE IV. — *The Same.   A Room in the Palace.*

Enter the Archbishop *of York, the young Duke of* YORK,
      Queen ELIZABETH, *and the* Duchess *of York.*

Arch. Last night, I hear, they lay at Northampton ;
At Stony-Stratford will they be to-night ;
To-morrow, or next day, they will be here.

Duch. I long with all my heart to see the Prince :
I hope he is much grown since last I saw him.

---

[3] If God *allot* or ordain it so.   *Sort* in the Latin sense of *sors.*
[4] *Reason,* again, for *talk* or *converse.*   See page 84, note 12.
[5] *Still,* here, is *always, continually.*   Often so.

Q. Eliz. But I hear, no; they say my son of York
Has almost overta'en him in his growth.

York. Ay, mother; but I would not have it so.

Duch. Why, my young cousin, it is good to grow.

York. Grandam, one night, as we did sit at supper,
My uncle Rivers talk'd how I did grow
More than my brother: *Ay,* quoth my uncle Gloster,
Small herbs have grace, great weeds do grow apace:
And since, methinks, I would not grow so fast,
Because sweet flowers are slow, and weeds make haste.

Duch. Good faith, good faith, the saying did not hold
In him that did object the same to thee:
He was the wretched'st thing when he was young,
So long a-growing and so leisurely,
That, if his rule were true, he should be gracious.

Arch. And so, no doubt, he is, my gracious madam.

Duch. I hope he is; but yet let mothers doubt.

York. Now, by my troth, if I had been remember'd,
I could have given my uncle's Grace a flout,
To touch his growth nearer than he touch'd mine.

Duch. How, my young York? I pr'ythee, let me hear it.

York. Marry, they say my uncle grew so fast
That he could gnaw a crust at two hours old:
'Twas full two years ere I could get a tooth.
Grandam, this would have been a biting jest.

Duch. I pr'ythee, pretty York, who told thee this?

York. Grandam, his nurse.

Duch. His nurse! why, she was dead ere thou wast born.

York. If 'twere not she, I cannot tell who told me.

Q. Eliz. A parlous[1] boy: — go to, you are too shrewd.

---

[1] *Parlous* is a popular form of *perilous;* jocularly used for *alarming.*

Arch. Good madam, be not angry with the child.

Q. Eliz. Pitchers have ears.

Arch. Here comes a messenger. —

Enter a Messenger.

What news?

Mess. Such news, my lord, as grieves me to report.

Q. Eliz. How doth the Prince?

Mess.   Well, madam, and in health.

Duch. What is thy news, then?

Mess. Lord Rivers and Lord Grey are sent to Pomfret,
With them Sir Thomas Vaughan, prisoners.

Duch. Who hath committed them?

Mess.   The mighty Dukes
Gloster and Buckingham.

Q. Eliz.   For what offence?

Mess. The sum of all I can i have disclosed:
Why or for what these nobles were committed
Is all unknown to me, my gracious lady.

Q. Eliz. Ah me, I see the downfall of our House!
The tiger now hath seized the gentle hind;
Insulting tyranny begins to jet
Upon the innocent and awless [2] throne:
Welcome, destruction, blood, and massacre!
I see, as in a map, the end of all.

Duch. Accursèd and unquiet wrangling days,
How many of you have mine eyes beheld!

---

[2] *To jet upon* means here *boldly to encroach upon.* So in *Titus Andronicus,* ii. 1: "And think you not how dangerous it is to *jet upon* a prince's
right?" And in an old manuscript play of *Sir Thomas More:* "It is hard
when Englishmens pacience must be thus *jetted on* by straungers. — *Awless*
is unreverenced, not looked upon with awe.

My husband lost his life to get the crown ;
And often up and down my sons were toss'd,
For me to joy and weep their gain and loss :
And, being seated, and domestic broils
Clean over-blown, themselves, the conquerors,
Make war upon themselves ; brother to brother,
Blood to blood, self against self : O, preposterous
And frantic outrage, end thy damnèd spleen ;
Or let me die, to look on death no more !

    Q. Eliz. Come, come, my boy ; we will to sanctuary. —
Madam, farewell.

    Duch.   Stay, I will go with you.

    Q. Eliz. You have no cause.

    Arch. [*To the* Queen.]   My gracious lady, go ;
And thither bear your treasure and your goods.
For my part, I'll resign unto your Grace
The seal I keep : and so betide to me
As well I tender you and all of yours !
Come, I'll conduct you to the sanctuary.   [*Exeunt.*

ACT III.

SCENE I. — *London. A Street.*

The trumpets sound. Enter the Prince of WALES, GLOSTER,
BUCKINGHAM, *Cardinal* BOURCHIER,[1] CATESBY, *and others.*

Buck. Welcome, sweet Prince, to London, to your chamber.[2]

Glos. Welcome, dear cousin, my thoughts' sovereign :
The weary way hath made you melancholy.

Prince. No, uncle ; but our crosses on the way
Have made it tedious, wearisome, and heavy :
I want more uncles here to welcome me.

Glos. Sweet Prince, th' untainted virtue of your years
Hath not yet dived into the world's deceit ;
Nor more can you distinguish of a man
Than of his outward show ; which, God he knows,
Seldom or never jumpeth[3] with the heart.
Those uncles which you want were dangerous ;
Your Grace attended to their sugar'd words,
But look'd not on the poison of their hearts :

---

[1] Thomas Bourchier was **made a** Cardinal, and elected Archbishop of
Canterbury in 1464.   He died in 1486.

[2] London was anciently called *camera regis,* that is, *the king's chamber.*
Thus in Buckingham's speech to the citizens as given by More : "The
prince, by *this noble citie as his speciall chamber,* and the speciall well re-
nowned citie of this realme, much honourable fame receiveth among all
other nations."

[3] To *jump* with is to *agree* or *correspond* with.   So in *1 King Henry IV.,*
i. 2 : "Well, Hal, well ; and in some sort it *jumps* with my humour."   See,
also, *The Merchant,* page 129, note 5.

God keep you from them, and from such false friends !

    Prince. God keep me from false friends ! but they were
      none.

    Glos. My lord, the Mayor of London comes to greet you.

Enter the Lord Mayor *and his Train.*

    May. God bless your Grace with health and happy days !

    Prince. I thank you, good my lord ; — and thank you
      all. —   [Mayor *and his Train retire.*

I thought my mother, and my brother York,

Would long ere this have met us on the way :

Fie, what a slug is Hastings, that he comes not

To tell us whether they will come or no !

    Buck. And, in good time, here comes the sweating lord.

Enter HASTINGS.

    Prince. Welcome, my lord : what, will our mother come ?

    Hast. On what occasion, God he knows, not I,

The Queen your mother, and your brother York,

Have taken sanctuary : the tender prince

Would fain have come with me to meet your Grace,

But by his mother was perforce withheld.

    Buck. Fie, what an indirect and peevish course

Is this of hers ! — Lord Cardinal, will your Grace

Persuade the Queen to send the Duke of York

Unto his princely brother presently ?

If she deny, — Lord Hastings, go with him,

And from her jealous arms pluck him perforce.

    Card. My Lord of Buckingham, if my weak oratory

Can from his mother win the Duke of York,

Anon expect him here ; but, if she be obdúrate

To mild entreaties, God in Heaven forbid

We should infringe the holy privilege

Of blessèd sanctuary ! not for all this land
Would I be guilty of so great a sin.

   Buck. You are too senseless-obstinate, my lord,
Too ceremonious and traditional ;[4]
Weigh it but with the grossness of this age.[5]
You break not sanctuary in seizing him :
The benefit thereof is always granted
To those whose dealings have deserved the place,
And those who have the wit to claim the place :
This Prince hath neither claim'd it nor deserved it ;
Therefore, in mine opinion, cannot have it :
Then, taking him from thence that is not there,
You break no privilege nor charter there.
Oft have I heard of sanctuary-men ;
But sanctuary-children ne'er till now.

   Card. My lord, you shall o'er-rule my mind for once. —
Come on, Lord Hastings, will you go with me ?

   Hast. I will, my lord.

   Prince. Good lords, make all the speedy haste you may. —

               [*Exeunt* Cardinal *and* HASTINGS.

Say, uncle Gloster, if our brother come,
Where shall we sojourn till our coronation ?

   Glos. Where it seems best unto your royal self.
If I may counsel you, some day or two

---

   4 *Ceremonious* for *superstitious*, or *tenacious of formalities; traditional*
for *adherent to received* customs.

   5 *Weigh* is in the same construction with *are* in the second line before,
the copulative *and* being understood. And to *weigh*, as the word is here
used, is to *judge* or to *consider*. So that the sense of the whole is, "You are
too much swayed by popular forms and traditions, and you judge the matter only in accordance with the gross and undistinguishing superstition
which now prevails." Such is, in substance, Heath's explanation of the
passage. See Critical Notes.

Your Highness shall repose you at the Tower;
Then where you please, and shall be thought most fit
For your best health and recreation.

Prince. I do not like the Tower, of any place. —
Did Julius Cæsar build that place, my lord?

Buck. He did, my gracious lord, begin that place;
Which, since, succeeding ages have re-edified.

Prince. Is it upon recórd, or else reported
Successively from age to age, he built it?

Buck. Upon recórd, my gracious lord.

Prince. But say, my lord, it were not register'd,
Methinks the truth should live from age to age,
As 'twere retail'd[6] to all posterity,
Even to the general all-ending day.

Glos. [*Aside.*] So wise so young, they say, do ne'er live
    long.

Prince. What say you, uncle?

Glos. I say, without charácters,[7] fame lives long. —
[*Aside.*] Thus, like the formal Vice,[8] Iniquity,

---

[6] That is, *recounted.* Minsheu, in his *Dictionary*, 1617, besides the verb *retail*, in the mercantile sense, has the verb to *retaile* or *retell.* Richard uses the word again in the fourth Act, when speaking to the Queen of her daughter: "To whom I will *retail* my conquests won."   *

[7] Without the help of *letters* or *inscriptions.* See *The Winter's Tale*, page 159, note 5.

[8] Of that distinguished personage, the Vice or Jester of the old Moralities, some account is given in *Twelfth Night*, p. 119, n. 17. His part appears to have been on all occasions much the same, consisting in a given round or *set form* of action; for which cause, probably, the epithet *formal* is here applied to him. The following is Gifford's description of him: "He appears to have been a perfect counterpart of the harlequin of the modern stage, and had a twofold office, — to instigate the hero of the piece to wickedness, and at the same time to protect him from the Devil, whom he was permitted to buffet and baffle with his wooden sword, till the process of the story required that both the protector and the protected should be carried

I moralize two meanings in one word.[9]

Prince. That Julius Cæsar was a famous man :
With what his valour did enrich his wit,
His wit set down to make his valour live :
Death makes no conquest of this conqueror ;
For now he lives in fame, though not in life. —
I'll tell you what, my cousin Buckingham, —

Buck. What, my gracious lord ?

Prince. An if I live until I be a man,
I'll win our ancient right in France again,
Or die a soldier, as I lived a king.

Glos. [*Aside.*] Short Summers lightly[10] have a forward
        Spring.

Buck. Now, in good time, here comes the Duke of York.

Enter YORK, *with the* Cardinal *and* HASTINGS.

Prince. Richard of York ! how fares our loving brother ?

York. Well, my dread lord ; so must I call you now.

Prince. Ay, brother, — to our grief, as it is yours :

---

off by the fiend ; or the latter driven roaring from the stage, by some
miraculous interposition in favour of the repentant offender."

[9] Heath explains as follows : "Thus my moralities, or the sententious
expressions I have just uttered, resemble those of the Vice, Iniquity, in the
play ; the indecencies which lie at the bottom are sheltered from exception
and the indignation they would excite if nakedly delivered, under the am-
biguity of a double meaning." The writer adds, "The term *moralize* is
only introduced in allusion to the title of our old dramatic pieces, which
were commonly called *Moralities*, in which the Vice was always one of the
shining characters." It is to be noted further, that, as the Vice acted the
part of a buffoon or jester, he was wont "to deal largely in double meanings, and by the help of them to aim at cracking a jest or raising a laugh."

[10] *Lightly*, here, is *commonly* or *usually*. So in an old proverb preserved
by Ray : "There's lightning *lightly* before thunder."

Too late [11] he died that might have kept that title,
Which by his death hath lost much majesty.

   Glos. How fares our cousin, noble Lord of York?

   York. I thank you, gentle uncle. O, my lord,
You said that idle weeds are fast in growth:
The Prince my brother hath outgrown me far.

   Glos. He hath, my lord.

   York.   And therefore is he idle?

   Glos. O, my fair cousin, I must not say so.

   York. Then is he more beholding to you than I.

   Glos. He may command me as my sovereign;
But you have power in me as in a kinsman.

   York. I pray you, uncle, give me this dagger.

   Glos. My dagger, little cousin? with all my heart.

   Prince. A beggar, brother?

   York. Of my kind uncle, that I know will give;
And being but a toy, which is no grief to give.

   Glos. A greater gift than that I'll give my cousin.

   York. A greater gift! O, that's the sword to it.

   Glos. Ay, gentle cousin, were it light enough.

   York. O, then, I see you'll part but with light gifts;
In weightier things you'll say a beggar nay.

   Glos. It is too heavy for your Grace to wear.

   York. I'd weigh it lightly, were it heavier. [12]

   Glos. What, would you have my weapon, little lord?

   York. I would, that I might thank you, as — as — you call
     me.

---

   [11] *Too late* for *too lately;* meaning, it is too short a time since his death,
not to be "to our grief, as it is yours."

   [12] York is playing on the word *lightly*, and means, in one sense, "I hold
it cheap," or "I care little for it." So in *Love's Labours Lost*, v. 2: "You
weigh me not! — O, that's you *care not* for me."

Glos. How?

York. Little.

Prince. My Lord of York will still be cross[13] in talk:
Uncle, your Grace knows how to bear with him.

York. You mean, to bear me, not to bear with me:—
Uncle, my brother mocks both you and me;
Because that I am little, like an ape,[14]
He thinks that you should bear me on your shoulders.

Buck. [*Aside to* HASTINGS.] With what a sharp-provided
      wit he reasons![15]
To mitigate the scorn he gives his uncle,
He prettily and aptly taunts himself:
So cunning and so young is wonderful.

Glos. My lord, will't please you pass along?
Myself and my good cousin Buckingham
Will to your mother, to entreat of her
To meet you at the Tower and welcome you.

York. What, will you go unto the Tower, my lord?

Prince. My Lord Protector needs will have it so.

York. I shall not sleep in quiet at the Tower.

Glos. Why, what should you fear?

York. Marry, my uncle Clarence' angry ghost:
My grandam told me he was murder'd there.

---

[13] *Cross* in a logical sense, not in a moral; *opposing*, or speaking at *cross-purposes;* taking him in a wrong sense.

[14] York alludes to the hump on Gloster's back, which was commodious for carrying burdens. So in Ulpian Fulwell's *Ars Adulandi*, 1576: "Thou hast an excellent *back* to carry my lord's ape."

[15] *Provided* seems to mean *furnished, pregnant, prompt;* or it may be an instance of the passive form with an active sense, *forecasting, provident.* We have the former sense in *well-provided,* which means *well-furnished* or *well-supplied.*— Here, again, *reasons* has the sense, apparently, of *talks* or *converses.* See page 103, note 4.

Prince. I fear no uncles dead.

Glos. Nor none that live, I hope.

Prince. An if they live, I hope I need not fear.
But come, my lord ; and with a heavy heart,
Thinking on them, go I unto the Tower.

   [*Sennet. Exeunt the* Prince, YORK, HASTINGS, Cardinal,
     and others ; also the Lord Mayor *and his Train.*

Buck. Think you, my lord, this little prating York
Was not incensèd by his subtle mother
To taunt and scorn you thus opprobriously ?

Glos. No doubt, no doubt : O, 'tis a parlous boy ;
Bold, quick, ingenious, forward, capable :
He's all the mother's, from the top to toe.

Buck. Well, let them rest.—Come hither, Catesby.   Thou
Art sworn as deeply to effect what we intend
As closely to conceal what we impart :
Thou know'st our reasons urged upon the way :
What think'st thou ? is it not an easy matter
To make William Lord Hastings of our mind,
For the instalment of this noble duke
In the seat royal of this famous isle !

Cate. He for his father's sake so loves the Prince,
That he will not be won to aught against him.

Buck. What think'st thou, then, of Stanley ? will not he ?

Cate. He will do all in all as Hastings doth.

Buck. Well, then no more but this : go, gentle Catesby,
And, as it were far off, sound thou Lord Hastings,
How he doth stand affected to our purpose ;
And summon him to-morrow to the Tower,
To sit about the coronation.
If thou dost find him tractable to us,
Encourage him, and show him all our reasons :

If he be leaden, icy-cold, unwilling,
Be thou so too ; and so break off your talk,
And give us notice of his inclination :
For we to-morrow hold divided Councils,
Wherein thyself shalt highly be employ'd.

   Glos. Commend me to Lord William : tell him, Catesby,
His ancient knot of dangerous adversaries
To-morrow are let blood at Pomfret-castle ;
And bid my friend, for joy of this good news,
Give Mistress Shore one gentle kiss the more.

   Buck. Good Catesby, go, effect this business soundly.

   Cate. My good lords both, with all the heed I can.

   Glos. Shall we hear from you, Catesby, ere we sleep?

   Cate. You shall, my lord.

   Glos. At Crosby-place, there shall you find us both.

                         [*Exit* CATESBY

   Buck. My lord, what shall we do, if we perceive
Lord Hastings will not yield to our complots?

   Glos. Chop off his head, man : somewhat we will do :
And, look, when I am king, claim thou of me
Th' earldom of Hereford, and the movables
Whereof the King my brother stood possess'd.

   Buck. I'll claim that promise at your Grace's hand.

   Glos. And look to have it yielded with all kindness.
Come, let us sup betimes, that afterwards
We may digest our complots in some form.

SCENE II. — *Before Lord* HASTINGS' *House.*

Enter a Messenger.

Mess. [*Knocking.*] My lord ! my lord ! —
Hast. [*Within.*] Who knocks?
Mess. One from the Lord Stanley.
Hast. [*Within.*] What is't o'clock?
Mess. Upon the stroke of four.

Enter HASTINGS.

Hast. Cannot thy master sleep these tedious nights?
Mess. So it appears by that I have to say.
First, he commends him to your noble self.
Hast. What then?
Mess. Then certifies your lordship, that this night
He dreamt the boar had rasèd[1] off his helm :
Besides, he says there are two Councils held ;
And that may be determined at the one
Which may make you and him to rue at th' other.
Therefore he sends to know your lordship's pleasure,
If presently you will take horse with him,
And with all speed post with him toward the North,
To shun the danger that his soul divines.
Hast. Go, fellow, go, return unto thy lord ;
Bid him not fear the separated Councils :
His Honour and myself are at the one,

---

[1] *Rased* or *rashed* was a term commonly used to describe the violence inflicted by a boar. Nott derives it from *Arracher*, French, to *root up*, to *draw, tear*, or *pull up*. So in *The Faerie Queene*, v. 3, 8 :

> There Marinell great deeds of armes did shew ;
> And through the thickest like a lyon flew,
> *Rashing off helmes*, and ryving plates asonder.

And at the other is my good friend Catesby;
Where nothing can proceed that toucheth us
Whereof I shall not have intelligence.
Tell him his fears are shallow, wanting instance:[2]
And for his dreams, I wonder he's so fond[3]
To trust the mockery of unquiet slumbers:
To fly the boar before the boar pursues,
Were to incense the boar to follow us,
And make pursuit where he did mean no chase.
Go, bid thy master rise and come to me;
And we will both together to the Tower,
Where he shall see the boar[4] will use us kindly.

 Mess. I'll go, my lord, and tell him what you say. [*Exit.*

Enter CATESBY.

 Cate. Many good morrows to my noble lord!
 Hast. Good morrow, Catesby; you are early stirring:
What news, what news, in this our tottering State?
 Cate. It is a reeling world, indeed, my lord;
And I believe will never stand upright
Till Richard wear the garland of the realm.
 Hast. How! wear the garland! dost thou mean the
  crown?
 Cate. Ay, my good lord.
 Hast. I'll have this crown of mine cut from my shoulders
Before I'll see the crown so foul misplaced.

---

 2 Without *example*, or without **any** matter-of-fact, to *instance*, or *allege in proof.* So in *The Merry Wives*, ii. 2, Ford says of his wife, "Now, could I come to her with any detection in my hand, my desires had *instance* and argument to commend themselves."

 3 *Fond*, here, as usual, is *foolish*, or *weak*.

 4 Of course the *boar* is Richard, whose crest was adorned with the figure of that amiable beast.

But canst thou guess that he doth aim at it?

Cate. Ay, on my life; and hopes to find you forward
Upon his party for the gain thereof:
And thereupon he sends you this good news,
That this same very day your enemies,
The kindred of the Queen, must die at Pomfret.

Hast. Indeed, I am no mourner for that news,
Because they have been still my adversaries:
But, that I'll give my voice on Richard's side,
To bar my master's heirs in true descent,
God knows I will not do it to the death.

Cate. God keep your lordship in that gracious mind!

Hast. But I shall laugh at this a twelve-month hence,
That they who brought me in my master's hate,
I live to look upon their tragedy.
Well, Catesby, ere a fortnight make me older,
I'll send some packing that yet think not on't.

Cate. 'Tis a vile thing to die, my gracious lord,
When men are unprepared and look not for it.

Hast. O monstrous, monstrous! and so falls it out
With Rivers, Vaughan, Grey: and so 'twill do
With some men else, that think themselves as safe
As thou and I; who, as thou know'st, are dear
To princely Richard and to Buckingham.

Cate. The princes both make high account of you,—
[*Aside.*] For they account his head upon the bridge.

Hast. I know they do; and I have well deserved it.—

Enter STANLEY.

Come on, come on; where is your boar-spear, man?
Fear you the boar, and go so unprovided?

Stan. My lord, good morrow;—good morrow, Catesby:—

You may jest on, but, by the holy Rood,[5]
I do not like these several Councils, I.

 Hast. My lord, I hold my life as dear as you do yours;
And never in my days, I do protest,
Was it more precious to me than 'tis now:
Think you, but that I know our state secure,
I would be so triumphant as I am?

 Stan. The lords at Pomfret, when they rode from London,
Were jocund, and supposed their states were sure;
And they, indeed, had no cause to mistrust;
But yet, you see, how soon the day o'ercast.
This sudden stab of rancour I misdoubt:
Pray God, I say, I prove a needless coward![6]
What, shall we toward the Tower? the day is spent.

 Hast. Come, come, have with you. Wot you what, my
   lord?
To-day the lords you talk of are beheaded.

 Stan. They, for their truth, might better wear their heads
Than some that have accused them wear their hats.
But come, my lord, let us away.

Enter a Pursuivant.[7]

 Hast. Go on before; I'll talk with this good fellow. —
       [*Exeunt* STANLEY *and* CATESBY.
How now, sirrah! how goes the world with thee?

---

5 "The *holy Rood*" is the *cross* or *crucifix*. A frequent oath.

6 To "prove a *needless* coward" here means, evidently, to prove a coward *needlessly* or *without cause*. Shakespeare has many instances of like
construction.

7 A *pursuivant* is now a State messenger, or one having authority to
execute warrants: the word formerly meant a junior officer of the Heralds'
College. In More's history this Pursuivant is spoken of as being also
named Hastings.

Purs. The better that your lordship please to ask.

Hast. I tell thee, man, 'tis better with me now
Than when thou mett'st me last where now we meet:
Then was I going prisoner to the Tower,
By the suggestion of the Queen's allies;
But now, I tell thee — keep it to thyself —
This day those enemies are put to death,
And I in better state than e'er I was.

Purs. God hold it,[8] to your Honour's good content!

Hast. Gramercy, fellow : there, drink that for me.

> [*Throwing him his purse.*

Purs. God save your lordship !   [*Exit.*

Enter a Priest.

Priest. Well met, my lord; I'm glad to see your Honour.

Hast. I thank thee, good Sir John, with all my heart.
I'm in your debt for your last exercise ;[9]
Come the next Sabbath, and I will content you.

Enter BUCKINGHAM.

Buck. What, talking with a priest, Lord Chamberlain !
Your friends at Pomfret, they do need the priest ;
Your Honour hath no shriving-work [10] in hand.

Hast. Good faith, and when I met this holy man,
The men you talk of came into my mind.
What, go you toward the Tower?

---

[8] " God *hold* it" is God *continue* it. — *Gramercy*, in the next line, is *great thanks;* from the French *grand merci.*

[9] *Exercise* here probably means *religious instruction.* — *Sir* was in common use as a clerical title. Thus we have *Sir* Oliver Martext in *As You Like It*, and *Sir* Hugh Evans in *The Merry Wives of Windsor.*

[10] *Shriving* or *shrift* is an old word for *confession* and *absolution.*

Buck. I do, my lord ; but long I cannot stay there :
I shall return before your lordship thence.

Hast. Nay, like enough, for I stay dinner there.

Buck. [*Aside.*] And supper too, although thou know'st it
not. —

Come, will you go?

Hast.   I'll wait upon your lordship. [*Exeunt.*

SCENE III. — *Pomfret. Before the Castle.*

Enter RATCLIFF, *with a Guard, conducting* RIVERS, GREY,
and VAUGHAN *to Execution.*

Riv. Sir Richard Ratcliff, let me tell thee this,
To-day shalt thou behold a subject die
For truth, for duty, and for loyalty.

Grey. God keep the Prince from all the pack of you !
A knot you are of damnèd blood-suckers.

Vaugh. You live that shall cry woe for this hereafter.

Rat. Dispatch ; the limit [1] of your lives is out.

Riv. O Pomfret, Pomfret ! O thou bloody prison,
Fatal and ominous to noble peers !
Within the guilty closure of thy walls
Richard the Second here was hack'd to death ;
And, for more slander to thy dismal seat,
We give thee up our guiltless blood to drink.

Grey. Now Margaret's curse is fall'n upon our heads,
When she exclaim'd on Hastings, you, and I,
For standing by when Richard stabb'd her son.

---

[1] *Limit*, here, is equivalent to *appointed time ;* to *appoint* being one of the
old meanings of to *limit*. So in *Measure for Measure*, iii. 1 : " Between
which time of the contract and *limit* of the solemnity," &c.

Riv. Then cursed she Richard, then cursed she Bucking-
  ham,
Then cursed she Hastings : — O, remember, God,
To hear her prayers for them, as now for us !
And, for my sister and her princely sons,
Be satisfied, dear God, with our true blood,
Which, as Thou know'st, unjustly must be spilt.
  Rat. Make haste ; the hour of death is expirate.[2]
  Riv. Come, Grey, — come, Vaughan, — let us here em-
  brace :
Farewell, until we meet again in Heaven.   [*Exeunt.*

SCENE IV. — *London.   A Room in the Tower.*

BUCKINGHAM, STANLEY, HASTINGS, *the Bishop of* ELY,[3] RAT-
CLIFF, LOVEL, *and others*, *sitting at a table ;* Officers *of the
Council attending.*

  Hast. Now, noble peers, the cause why we are met
Is, to determine of the coronation.
In God's name, speak ; when is the royal day?
  Buck. Are all things ready for that royal time?
  Stan. They are ; and wants but nomination.[4]
  Ely. To-morrow, then, I judge a happy [5] day.

  [2] *Expirate* for *expired*, that is, *expired*. So, before, *convict* for *convicted*. See page 85, note 14.
  [3] Dr. John Morton, who was elected to the see of Ely in 1478. He was
advanced to the see of Canterbury in 1486, and appointed Lord Chancellor
in 1487. He died in the year 1500. This prelate first devised the scheme
of putting an end to the long contest between the Houses of York and Lancaster, by a marriage between Henry Earl of Richmond and Elizabeth, the
eldest daughter of Edward IV.; and was a principal agent in bringing that
arrangement about.
  [4] And there wants or is wanting but a *naming of the time.*
  [5] *Happy* here means *auspicious*, the same as the Latin *felix.*

Buck. Who knows the Lord Protector's mind herein?
Who is most inward [6] with the noble duke?

Ely. Your Grace, we think, should soonest know his mind.

Buck. We know each other's faces: for our hearts,
He knows no more of mine than I of yours;
Nor I of his, my lord, than you of mine. —
Lord Hastings, you and he are near in love.

Hast. I thank his Grace, I know he loves me well;
But, for his purpose in the coronation,
I have not sounded him, nor he deliver'd
His gracious pleasure any way therein: .
But you, my noble lords, may name the time;
And in the duke's behalf I'll give my voice,
Which, I presume, he'll take in gentle part.

Ely. In happy time, here comes the duke himself.

Enter GLOSTER.

Glos. My noble lords and cousins all, good morrow.
I have been long a sleeper: but, I trust,
My absence doth neglect no great design,
Which by my presence might have been concluded.

Buck. Had you not come upon your cue, [7] my lord,
William Lord Hastings had pronounced your part, —
I mean, your voice, — for crowning of the King.

Glos. Than my Lord Hastings no man might be bolder;
His lordship knows me well, and loves me well. —
My Lord of Ely, when I was last in Holborn,

---

[6] *Inward*, as here used, is *intimate* or *confidential*. The same word occurs as a substantive with the same sense in *Measure for Measure*, iii. 2:
" Sir, I was *an inward* of his."

[7] An expression borrowed from the stage: the *cue*, *queue*, or *tail* of a speech being the last words, and so indicating to the next speaker when to *take his turn*.

I saw good strawberries in your garden there :
I do beseech you send for some of them.[8]

   Ely. Marry, and will, my lord, with all my heart.   [*Exit.*

   Glos. Cousin of Buckingham, a word with you.

                              [*Takes him aside.*

Catesby hath sounded Hastings in our business,
And finds the testy gentleman so hot,
That he will lose his head ere give consent
His master's child, as worshipfully he terms it,
Shall lose the royalty of England's throne.

   Buck. Withdraw you hence, my lord ; I'll follow you.

           [*Exit* GLOSTER, *followed by* BUCKINGHAM.

   Stan. We have not yet set down this day of triumph.
To-morrow, in my judgment, is too sudden ;
For I myself am not so well provided
As else I would be, were the day prolong'd.

Re-enter the Bishop of ELY.

   Ely. Where is my lord the Duke of Gloster?
I have sent for these strawberries.

   Hast. His Grace looks cheerfully and smooth to-day ;
There's some conceit or other likes[9] him well,

---

[8] This easy affability and smoothness of humour when going about the blackest and bloodiest crimes is one of the most telling strokes in this terrible portrait.   The incident is thus related in the History : " These lords so sitting togither communing of this matter, the protector came in amongst them first about nine of the clocke, saluting them courteouslie, and excusing himselfe that had been from them so long, saieng merilie that he had beene a sleeper that daie.   After a little talking with them he said unto the bishop of Elie, My lord, you have verie good strawberies at your garden in Holborne ; I require you, let us have a messe of them.   Gladlie, my lord, quoth he ; would God I had some better thing as readie to your pleasure as that ! And therewithall in all hast he sent his servant for a messe of strawberies."

[9] Some *thought* or *conception* that *pleases* him well.   *Conceit* is generally so in old writers, and *likes* very often so.

When he doth bid good-morrow with such spirit.
I think there's ne'er a man in Christendom
Can lesser hide his love or hate than he;
For by his face straight shall you know his heart.

Stan. What of his heart perceive you in his face
By any likelihood he show'd to-day?

Hast. Marry, that with no man here he's offended;
For, were he, he had shown it in his looks.

Re-enter GLOSTER *and* BUCKINGHAM.

Glos. I pray you all, tell me what they deserve
That do conspire my death with devilish plots
Of damnèd witchcraft, and that have prevail'd
Upon my body with their hellish charms?

Hast. The tender love I bear your Grace, my lord,
Makes me most forward in this noble presence
To doom th' offenders: whosoe'er they be,
I say, my lord, they have deservèd death.

Glos. Then be your eyes the witness of their evil:
Look how I am bewitch'd; behold mine arm
Is, like a blasted sapling, wither'd up:
And this is Edward's wife, that monstrous witch,
Consorted with that harlot-woman Shore,
That by their witchcraft thus have markèd me.

Hast. If they have done this thing, my gracious lord, —

Glos. If! thou protector of this damnèd harlot,
Talk'st thou to me of *ifs?*   Thou art a traitor: —
Off with his head! now, by Saint Paul, I swear
I will not dine until I see the same. —
Lovel and Ratcliff,[10] look that it be done: —

---

[10] In the preceding scene, we have Ratcliff at Pomfret, conducting Rivers,
Grey, and Vaughan to death; yet the events of that scene and this are rep-

The rest, that love me, rise and follow me.

          [*Exeunt all but* HASTINGS, LOVEL, *and* RATCLIFF.

  Hast. Woe, woe for England ! not a whit for me ;
For I, too fond, might have prevented this.
Stanley did dream the boar did rase his helm ;
But I disdain'd it, and did scorn to fly :
Three times to-day my foot-cloth horse [11] did stumble,
And started when he look'd upon the Tower,
As loth to bear me to the slaughter-house.
O, now I need the priest that spake to me :
I now repent I told the pursuivant,
As too triúmphing, how mine enemies
To-day at Pomfret bloodily were butcher'd,
And I myself secure in grace and favour. —
O Margaret, Margaret, now thy heavy curse
Is lighted on poor Hastings' wretched head !

  Rat. Dispatch, my lord ; the duke would be at dinner :
Make a short shrift ; he longs to see your head.

  Hast. O momentary grace of mortal men,
Which we more hunt for than the grace of God !
Who builds his hope in air of your fair looks,
Lives like a drunken sailor on a mast,
Ready, with every nod, to tumble down
Into the fatal bowels of the deep.

  Lov. Come, come, dispatch ; 'tis bootless to exclaim.

resented as occurring the same day. Knight thinks "this is one of those positions in which the Poet has trusted to the imagination of his audience rather than to their topographical knowledge." It may be so, but it seems to me much more likely to have been a simple oversight on the Poet's part.

  [11] A *foot-cloth* was a kind of housing that covered the body of the horse, and reached nearly to the ground. A *foot-cloth horse* was a palfrey covered with such housings, used for state ; and was the usual mode of conveyance for the rich, at a period when carriages were unknown.

Hast. O bloody Richard ! — miserable England !
I prophesy the fearfull'st time to thee
That ever wretched age hath look'd upon. —
Come, lead me to the block ; bear him my head :
They smile at me who shortly shall be dead.[12]   [*Exeunt.*

Scene V. — *The Same.   The Tower-walls.*

Enter Gloster *and* Buckingham, *in rusty armour, marvellous ill-favoured.*

Glos. Come, cousin, canst thou quake, and change thy
    colour,
Murder thy breath in middle of a word,
And then begin again, and stop again,
As if thou wert distraught[1] and mad with terror?
Buck. Tut, I can counterfeit the deep tragedian ;
Speak and look back, and pry on every side,
Tremble and start at wagging of a straw,
Intending[2] deep suspicion : ghastly looks
Are at my service, like enforcèd smiles ;
And both are ready in their offices,
At any time, to grace my stratagems.

[12] William Lord Hastings was beheaded on the 13th of June, 1483. His eldest son by Catharine Neville, daughter of Richard Neville, Earl of Salisbury, and widow of William Lord Bonville, was restored to his honours and estate by King Henry VII. in the first year of his reign.

[1] *Distraught* is an old form of *distracted.*

[2] *Intend* is repeatedly used by Shakespeare for *pretend.* So, again, in the seventh scene of this Act : "*Intend* some fear." Also, in *Lucrece :* "For then is Tarquin brought unto his bed, *intending* weariness with heavy sprite." On the other hand, the Poet repeatedly has *pretend* and its derivatives in the sense of *intend.* See, also, *Much Ado,* page 56, note 2.

But what, is Catesby gone?

Glos. He is; and, see, he brings the Mayor along.

Buck. Let me alone to entertain him. —

Enter the Lord Mayor and CATESBY.

Lord Mayor, —

Glos. Look to the drawbridge there!

Buck.   Hark! a drum.

Glos. Catesby, o'erlook the walls.

Buck. Lord Mayor, the reason we have sent for you, —

Glos. Look back, defend thee; here are enemies.

Buck. God and our innocence defend and guard us!

Glos. Be patient, they are friends, Ratcliff and Lovel.

Enter LOVEL and RATCLIFF, with HASTINGS' head.

Lov. Here is the head of that ignoble traitor,
The dangerous and unsuspected Hastings.

Glos. So dear I loved the man, that I must weep.
I took him for the plainest harmless creature
That breathed upon the Earth a Christian;
Made him my book, wherein my soul recorded
The history of all her secret thoughts:
So smooth he daub'd[3] his vice with show of virtue,
That, his apparent open guilt omitted, —
I mean, his conversation[4] with Shore's wife, —
He lived from all attainder of suspect.[5]

Buck. Well, well, he was the covert'st shelter'd traitor

---

[3] To *daub* was used for to *disguise*, to *cover over*. So in *King Lear*, iv. 1:
" I cannot *daub* it further."

[4] Familiar intercourse; what is now called *criminal conversation.* —
Apparent, again, in the sense of *manifest.* See page 100, note 15.

[5] *Suspect* for *suspicion.* So, before, in i. 3: " You do me shameful injury,
falsely to draw me in these vile *suspects.*"

That ever lived. —
Would you imagine, or almost believe, —
Were't not that, by great preservation,
We live to tell it you, — the subtle traitor
This day had plotted, in the Council-house,
To murder me and my good Lord of Gloster?

    May. What, had he so?

    Glos. What, think you we are Turks or infidels?
Or that we would, against the form of law,
Proceed thus rashly in the villain's death,
But that the éxtreme peril of the case,
The peace of England and our persons' safety,
Enforced us to this execution?

    May. Now, fair befall you! he deserved his death;
And your good Graces both have well proceeded,
To warn false traitors from the like attempts.
I never look'd for better at his hands,
After he once fell in with Mistress Shore.

    Buck. Yet had we not determined he should die,
Until your lordship came to see his end;
Which now the loving haste of these our friends,
Somewhat against our meaning, have [6] prevented;
Because, my lord, we would have had you hear
The traitor speak, and timorously confess
The manner and the purpose of his treason;
That you might well have signified the same
Unto the citizens, who haply may
Misconstrue us in him, and wail his death.

    May. But, my good lord, your Grace's word shall serve,

---

[6] Properly it should be *has*. But the old writers have many such instances where the verb is made to agree with the nearest substantive, as with *friends* here, instead of its proper subject.

As well as I had seen, and heard him speak;
And do not doubt, right noble princes both,
But I'll acquaint our duteous citizens
With all your just proceedings in this case.

Glos. And to that end we wish'd your lordship here,
T' avoid the censures of the carping world.

Buck. But since you come too late of[7] our intent,
Yet witness what you hear we did intend:
And so, my good Lord Mayor, we bid farewell.

[Exit Lord Mayor.

Glos. Go, after, after, cousin Buckingham.
The Mayor towards Guildhall hies him in all post:
There, at your meetest vantage of the time,
Infer[8] the bastardy of Edward's children:
Tell them how Edward put to death a citizen,
Only for saying he would make his son
Heir to the crown; meaning, indeed, his house,
Which, by the sign thereof, was termèd so.[9]
Moreover, urge his hateful luxury,
And bestial appetite in change of lust;
Which stretch'd unto their servants, daughters, wives,
Even where his raging eye or savage heart,
Without control, listed to make a prey.

Buck. Doubt not, my lord, I'll play the orator

---

[7] In common speech a similar phrase is used, " to come *short of* a thing."

[8] *Infer* is here used in the sense of *introduce* or *bring forward;* one of its Latin senses. So in iv. 4, of this play: " *Infer* fair England's peace by this alliance."

[9] This person was one *Walker,* a substantial citizen and grocer, at the *Crown* in Cheapside. These topics of Edward's cruelty, lust, unlawful marriage, &c., are enlarged upon in that most extraordinary invective, the petition presented to Richard before his accession, which was afterwards turned into an Act of Parliament.

As if the golden fee for which I plead
Were for myself : and so, my lord, adieu.

    Glos. If you thrive well, bring them to Baynard's Castle ; [10]
Where you shall find me well accompanied
With reverend fathers and well-learnèd bishops.

    Buck. I go ; and towards three or four o'clock
Look for the news that the Guildhall affords.   [*Exit.*

    Glos. Go, Lovel, with all speed to Doctor Shaw,—
[*To* CATE.] Go thou to Friar Penker : [11]—bid them both
Meet me within this hour at Baynard's Castle.—

                [*Exeunt* LOVEL, CATESBY, *and* RATCLIFF.
Now will I in, to take some privy order,
To draw the brats of Clarence out of sight ;
And to give notice that no manner person [12]
Have any time recourse unto the Princes.   [*Exit.*

   [10] This castle was built by Baynard, a nobleman who is said to have come in with William the Conqueror. It stood on the bank of the river in Thames-street, but has been swept away by the commercial necessities of London.

   [11] Dr. Shaw was brother to the Lord Mayor; Penker, according to Speed, was provincial of the Augustine friars; and both were popular preachers of the time.

   [12] The expression "no manner person" is according to the idiom of the time. — "The brats of Clarence" were Edward and Margaret, known afterwards as Earl of Warwick and Countess of Salisbury.

SCENE VI. — *The Same.   A Street.*

Enter a Scrivener.[1]

Scriv. Here is th' indictment of the good Lord Hastings;
Which in a set hand fairly is engross'd,[2]
That it may be to-day read o'er in Paul's.
And mark how well the sequel hangs together:
Eleven hours I have spent to write it over,
For yesternight by Catesby was it sent me;
The precedent[3] was full as long a-doing:
And yet within these five hours Hastings lived,
Untainted, unexamined, free, at liberty.
Here's a good world the while!   Why, who's so gross
That cannot see this palpable device?
Yet who so bold but says he sees it not?
Bad is the world; and all will come to naught
When such ill dealing must be seen in thought.[4]   [*Exit.*

---

[1] A *scrivener* is, literally, a *writer* or a *scribe*. The term was applied to a class of men whose special business it was to draw up or to transcribe legal writings and instruments.

[2] To *engross*, as the word is here used, is to copy legal or other documents in a clear, legible hand for public use. — In the olden time, St. Paul's Cathedral was used as a sort of exchange, and all sorts of notices were posted there for the public eye.   The edifice was not used in Shakespeare's time, it having been set on fire by a stroke of lightning and the roof burnt off early in Elizabeth's reign.   The present St. Paul's was not built till the time of Charles the Second.

[3] The original draft from which the copy was made.

[4] "Seen in *thought* is seen in *silence*." — I am not certain whether the last word of the preceding line should be *nought* or *naught*. With the latter, the sense is about the same as in our phrase of "going to the *bad*." See page 50, note 17.

SCENE VII. — *The Same.　Court of Baynard's Castle.*

Enter GLOSTER *and* BUCKINGHAM, *meeting.*

Glos.　How now, how now ! what say the citizens?

Buck.　Now, by the holy Mother of our Lord,
The citizens are mum, say not a word.

Glos.　Touch'd you the bastardy of Edward's children?

Buck.　I did; with his contráct with Lady Lucy,[5]
And his contráct by deputy in France ;
Th' insatiate greediness of his desires ;
His tyranny for trifles ; his own bastardy :[6]
Withal I did infer[7] your lineaments,
Being the right idea[8] of your father,
Both in your form and nobleness of mind ;
Laid open all your victories in Scotland,
Your discipline in war, wisdom in peace,
Your bounty, virtue, fair humility ;
Indeed, left nothing fitting for the purpose
Untouch'd, or slightly handled, in discourse :

---

[5] The King had been familiar with this lady before his marriage with the present Queen, to obstruct which his mother alleged a precontract between them. But Elizabeth Lucy, being sworn to speak the truth, declared that the King had not been affianced to her. Edward, however, had been married to Lady Eleanor Butler, widow of Lord Butler of Sudley, and daughter to the great Earl of Shrewsbury. On this ground his children were declared illegitimate by the only Parliament convened by Richard; but nothing was said of Elizabeth Lucy.

[6] This tale is supposed to have been first propagated by the Duke of Clarence when he obtained a settlement of the crown on himself and his issue after the death of Henry VI. Sir Thomas More says that the Duke of Gloster, soon after Edward's death, revived this scandal.

[7] *Infer* again as explained in note 8, page 130.

[8] *Idea* is here used in the right classic sense of *image* or *likeness.*

And, when my oratory drew toward end,
I bade them that did love their country's good
Cry, *God save Richard, England's royal King!*

   Glos. And did they so?

   Buck. No, so God help me, they spake not a word;
But, like dumb statuas [9] or breathing stones,
Stared each on other, and look'd deadly pale.
Which when I saw, I reprehended them;
And ask'd the Mayor what meant this wilful silence:
His answer was, The people were not used
To be spoke to but by the récorder.
Then he was urged to tell my tale again:
Thus saith the duke, thus hath the duke inferr'd;
But nothing spake in warrant from himself.
When he had done, some followers of mine own,
At lower end o' the hall, hurl'd up their caps,
And some ten voices cried, *God save King Richard!*
And thus I took the vantage of those few:
Thanks, gentle citizens and friends, quoth I;
This general applause and cheerful shout
Argues your wisdom and your love to Richard:
And even here brake off, and came away.

   Glos. What tongueless blocks were they! would they not
     speak?

   Buck. No, by my troth, my lord.

   Glos. Will not the Mayor, then, and his brethren, come?

   Buck. The Mayor is here at hand.   Intend some fear;
Be not you spoke with but by mighty suit:
And look you get a Prayer-book in your hand,
And stand between two churchmen,[10] good my lord;

---

   9 *Statue* was very often written and printed *statua*, as a trisyllable.

   10 *Churchmen* was formerly used of what are now called clergymen.

For on that ground I'll make a holy descant : [11]
And be not easily won to our request ;
Play the maid's part ; still answer nay, and take it.

   Glos. I go ; and if you plead as well for them
As I can say nay to thee for myself,
No doubt we'll bring it to a happy issue.

   Buck. Go, go, up to the leads ; [12] the Lord Mayor knocks. —
                                  [Exit GLOSTER.

Enter the Lord Mayor, Aldermen, *and* Citizens.

Welcome, my lord : I dance attendance here ;
I think the duke will not be spoke withal. —

Enter, from the Castle, CATESBY.

Now, Catesby, what says your lord to my request?

   Cate. He doth entreat your Grace, my noble lord,
To visit him to-morrow or next day :
He is within, with two right-reverend fathers,
Divinely bent to meditation ;
And in no worldly suit would he be moved,
To draw him from his holy exercise.

   Buck. Return, good Catesby, to the gracious duke ;
Tell him, myself, the Mayor and Aldermen,
In deep designs and matters of great moment,
No less importing than our general good,
Are come to have some conference with his Grace.

   Cate. I'll signify so much unto him straight.   *[Exit.*

---

   11 *Ground* and *descant* were technical terms in music; the former meaning the original air, the latter the variations.

   12 Formerly many buildings were roofed with lead. "Up to the *leads*" therefore means up to the *roof,* or close under the *eaves;* the topmost part of the building.

Buck. Ah, ha, my lord, this prince is not an Edward !
He is not lolling on a lewd day-bed,
But on his knees at meditation ;
Not dallying with a brace of courtezans,
But meditating with two deep divines ;
Not sleeping, to engross [13] his idle body,
But praying, to enrich his watchful soul.
Happy were England, would this virtuous prince
Take on himself the sovereignty thereof ;
But sore I fear we shall not win him to it.

   May. Marry, God defend his Grace should say us nay !

   Buck. I fear he will.   Here Catesby comes again. —

Re-enter CATESBY.

Now, Catesby, what says his Grace ?

   Cate. He wonders to what end you have assembled
Such troops of citizens to come to him,
His Grace not being warn'd thereof before :
He fears, my lord, you mean no good to him.

   Buck. Sorry I am my noble cousin should
Suspect me, that I mean no good to him :
By Heaven, we come to him in perfect love ;
And so once more return and tell his Grace. —

                         [*Exit* CATESBY

When holy and devout religious men
Are at their beads, 'tis much to draw them thence ;
So sweet is zealous contemplation.

Enter GLOSTER, *in a gallery above, between two* Bishops.
CATESBY *returns.*

   May. See, where his Grace stands 'tween two clergymen !

---

[13] That is, to pamper, fatten, or *make gross.*

Buck. Two props of virtue for a Christian prince,
To stay him from the fall of vanity :
And, see, a book of prayer [14] in his hand, —
True ornament to know a holy man. —
Famous Plantagenet, most gracious prince,
Lend favourable ear to our request ;
And pardon us the interruption
Of thy devotion and right Christian zeal.

Glos. My lord, there needs no such apology :
I rather do beseech you pardon me,
Who, earnest in the service of my God,
Neglect the visitation of my friends.
But, leaving this, what is your Grace's pleasure ?

Buck. Even that, I hope, which pleaseth God above,
And all good men of this ungovern'd isle.

Glos. I do suspect I have done some offence
That seems disgracious in the city's eye ;
And that you come to reprehend my ignorance.

Buck. You have, my lord : would it might please your
          Grace,
On our entreaties, to amend your fault !

Glos. Else wherefore breathe I in a Christian land ?

Buck. Know, then, it is your fault that you resign
The supreme seat, the throne majestical,
The scepter'd office of your ancestors,
Your state of fortune and your due of birth,
The lineal glory of your royal House,
To the corruption of a blemish'd stock :
Whilst, in the mildness of your sleepy thoughts, —

---

14 *Prayer* is used by Shakespeare as one or two syllables indifferently,
to suit his verse. Here it is a dissyllable. The same of *hour, fire, even,
given, power, flower, toward* or *towards,* and sundry others.

Which here we waken to our country's good,—
This noble isle doth want her proper limbs;
Her face defaced with scars of infamy,
Her royal stock graft with ignoble plants,
And almost shoulder'd in [15] the swallowing gulf
Of dark forgetfulness and deep oblivion.
Which to recure,[16] we heartily solicit
Your gracious self to take on you the charge
And kingly government of this your land;
Not as protector, steward, substitute,
Or lowly factor for another's gain;
But as successively, from blood to blood,
Your right of birth, your empery, your own.
For this, consorted with the citizens,
Your very worshipful and loving friends,
And by their vehement instigation,
In this just suit come I to move your Grace.

   Glos. I cannot tell, if to depart in silence,
Or bitterly to speak in your reproof,
Best fitteth my degree or your condition:
If not to answer, you might haply think
Tongue-tied ambition, not replying, yielded
To bear the golden yoke of sovereignty,

---

[15] *In* for *into*, the two being often used indiscriminately.—To *shoulder*, as the word is here used, is to *thrust* or *heave* by force or violence. Steevens quotes a similar expression from Lyson's *Environs of London :* " Lyke tyraunts and lyke madde men helpynge to *shulderynge* other of the sayd bannermen ynto the dyche." — In the preceding line, *graft* for *grafted*, as before *convict* for *convicted*. See page 85, note 14.

[16] To *recure* is to *recover*. Spenser has the word repeatedly in the same sense. So *The Faerie Queene*, ii. 12, 19:

> Whose mariners and merchants with much toyle
> Labour'd in vaine to have *recur'd* their prize.

Which fondly you would here impose on me ;
If to reprove you for this suit of yours,
So season'd with your faithful love to me,
Then, on the other side, I check'd my friends.
Therefore,—to speak, and to avoid the first,
And then, in speaking, not t' incur the last,—
Definitively thus I answer you.
Your love deserves my thanks ; but my desert
Unmeritable [17] shuns your high request.
First, if all obstacles were cut away,
And that my path were even to the crown,
As the ripe révenue and due of birth ;
Yet so much is my poverty of spirit,
So mighty and so many my defects,
That I would rather hide me from my greatness—
Being a bark to brook no mighty sea—
Than in my greatness covet to be hid,
And in the vapour of my glory smother'd.
But, God be thank'd, there is no need of me ;
And much I need, to help you, were there need : [18]
The royal tree hath left us royal fruit,
Which, mellow'd by the stealing hours of time,
Will well become the seat of majesty,
And make, no doubt, us happy by his reign.
On him I lay what you would lay on me,
The right and fortune of his happy stars ;
Which God defend [19] that I should wring from him !

[17] *Unmeritable* for *unmeriting*. This indiscriminate use of active and passive forms occurs very often.

[18] "And I fall far short of the ability to help you, if help were needed."

[19] "God *defend*" is the same as God *forbid*. Repeatedly used thus by Shakespeare ; and a common usage of the time.

Buck. My lord, this argues conscience in your Grace;
But the respects thereof are nice[20] and trivial,
All circumstances well consideréd.
You say that Edward is your brother's son:
So say we too, but not by Edward's wife;
For first he was contráct to Lady Lucy,—
Your mother lives a witness to his vow,—
And afterward by substitute betroth'd
To Bona, sister to the King of France.
These both put by, a poor petitioner,
A care-crazed mother of a many children,
A beauty-waning and distressèd widow,
Even in the afternoon of her best days,
Made prize and purchase of his wanton eye,
Seduced the pitch and height of his degree
To base declension and loathed bigamy.
More bitterly could I expostulate,
Save that, for reverence to some alive,[21]
I give a sparing limit to my tongue.
Then, good my lord, take to your royal self
This proffer'd benefit of dignity;
If not to bless us and the land withal,
Yet to draw forth your noble ancestry
From the corruption of abusing time
Unto a lineal true-derivèd course.

    May. Do, good my lord; your citizens entreat you.
    Buck. Refuse not, mighty lord, this proffer'd love.

---

[20] *Respects* for *considerations;* a frequent sense of the word. — *Nice* here means *unimportant,* or, perhaps, *over-scrupulous.*

[21] Buckingham here hints at the pretended illegitimacy of Edward and Clarence. By "some alive" he means the Duchess of York, the mother of Edward and Richard.

Cate. O, make them joyful, grant their lawful suit !

Glos. Alas, why would you heap those cares on me?
I am unfit for state and majesty.
I do beseech you, take it not amiss ;
I cannot nor I will not yield to you.

Buck. If you refuse it, — as, in love and zeal,
Loth to depose the child, your brother's son ;
As well we know your tenderness of heart,
And gentle, kind, effeminate remorse,[22]
Which we have noted in you to your kindred,
And equally indeed to all estates ; —
Yet, whether you accept our suit or no,
Your brother's son shall never reign our King ;
But we will plant some other in the throne,
To the disgrace and downfall of your House :
And in this resolution here we leave you. —
Come, citizens : zounds ! I'll entreat no more.

Glos. O, do not swear, my Lord of Buckingham.

[*Exit* BUCKINGHAM : *the* Mayor, Aldermen, *and*
Citizens *retiring.*

Cate. Call them again, sweet prince, accept their suit :
If you deny them, all the land will rue it.

Glos. Will you enforce me to a world of cares?
Call them again.

[CATESBY *goes to the* Mayor, *&c., and then exit.*
— I am not made of stone,
But penetrable to your kind entreats,
Albeit against my conscience and my soul. —

Re-enter BUCKINGHAM *and* CATESBY ; *the* Mayor, *&c., coming
forward.*

---

22 *Remorse*, again, for *pity* or *compassion*. See page 59, note 16.

Cousin of Buckingham, — and sage, grave men, —
Since you will buckle fortune on my back,
To bear her burden, whêr I will or no,
I must have patience to endure the load :
But, if black scandal or foul-faced reproach
Attend the sequel of your imposition,
Your mere enforcement shall acquittance [23] me
From all the impure blots and stains thereof ;
For God he knows, and you may partly see,
How far I am from the desire of this.

 May. God bless your Grace ! we see it, and will say it.

 Glos. In saying so, you shall but say the truth.

 Buck. Then I salute you with this royal title :
Long live King Richard, England's worthy King !

 Mayor, &c. Amen.

 Buck. To-morrow may it please you to be crown'd ?

 Glos. Even when you please, since you will have it so.

 Buck. To-morrow, then, we will attend your Grace :
And so, most joyfully, we take our leave.

 Glos. [*To the* Bishops.] Come, let us to our holy work
  again. —
Farewell, good cousin ; — farewell, gentle friends. [*Exeunt.*

---

[23] *Acquittance* for *acquit*, because the verse wanted a trisyllable.

ACT IV.

SCENE I. — *London.   Before the Tower.*

Enter, on one side, Queen ELIZABETH, *Duchess of* YORK, *and*
DORSET ; *on the other,* ANNE *Duchess of* GLOSTER,[1] *leading
Lady* MARGARET PLANTAGENET, CLARENCE'S *young Daughter.*

Duch. Who meets us here? my niece [2] Plantagenet,
Led in the hand of her kind aunt of Gloster?
Now, for my life, she's wandering to the Tower,
On pure heart's love, to greet the tender Princes. —
Daughter, well met.

Anne.   God give your Graces both
A happy and a joyful time of day !

Q. Eliz. As much to you, good sister !   Whither away?

Anne. No further than the Tower ; and, as I guess,
Upon the like devotion as yourselves,
To gratulate the gentle Princes there.

Q. Eliz. Kind sister, thanks : we'll enter all together :
And, in good time, here the lieutenant comes. —

Enter BRAKENBURY.

Master lieutenant, pray you, by your leave,

---

1 We have not seen this lady since the second scene of the first Act, in
which she promised to meet Richard at Crosby-place. She was marrried to
him about the year 1472.

2 The Duchess is speaking to what we should call her grand-daughter.
But the words *grand-son, grand-daughter, grand-children*, are not used by
Shakespeare at all ; their places being supplied by *nephew* and *niece ;* sometimes by *cousin.*

How doth the Prince, and my young son of York?

Brak. Right well, dear madam.   By your patience,
I may not suffer you to visit them ;
The King hath straitly charged the contrary.

Q. Eliz. The King ! who's that?

Brak.   I mean the Lord Protector.

Q. Eliz. The Lord protect him from that kingly title !
Hath he set bounds between their love and me ?
I am their mother ; who shall bar me from them ?

Duch. I am their father's mother ; I will see them.

Anne. Their aunt I am in law, in love their mother :
Then bring me to their sights ; I'll bear thy blame,
And take thy office from thee, on my peril.

Brak. No, madam, no ; I may not leave it so : [3]
I'm bound by oath, and therefore pardon me.   [*Exit.*

Enter STANLEY.

Stan. Let me but meet you, ladies, one hour hence,
And I'll salute your Grace of York as mother,
And reverend looker-on, of two fair queens. —
[*To* ANNE.] Come, madam, you must straight to Westminster,
There to be crownèd Richard's royal Queen.

Q. Eliz. Ah, cut my lace asunder,
That my pent heart may have some scope to beat,
Or else I swoon with this dead-killing news !

Anne. Despiteful tidings !   O unpleasing news !

Dor. Be of good cheer :—mother, how fares your Grace ?

Q. Eliz. O Dorset, speak not to me, get thee hence !
Death and destruction dog thee at the heels ;
Thy mother's name is ominous to children.

---

[3] He refers to his office or charge, which she has offered to take upon
herself at her own risk or peril.

If thou wilt outstrip death, go cross the seas,
And live with Richmond, from the reach of Hell:
Go, hie thee, hie thee from this slaughter-house,
Lest thou increase the number of the dead;
And make me die the thrall of Margaret's curse,
Nor mother, wife, nor England's counted Queen.

Stan. Full of wise care is this your counsel, madam. —
Take all the swift advantage of the hours;
You shall have letters from me to my son
In your behalf, to meet you on the way:
Be not ta'en tardy by unwise delay.

Duch. O ill-dispersing wind of misery! —
O my accursèd womb, the bed of death!
A cockatrice[4] hast thou hatch'd to the world,
Whose unavoided eye is murderous.

Stan. Come, madam, come; I in all haste was sent.

Anne. And I in all unwillingness will go. —
O, would to God that the inclusive verge
Of golden metal that must round my brow
Were red-hot steel, to sear me to the brain![5]

---

[4] The *cockatrice* was so called from its fabled generation from the egg of a cock; the term being derived from *cock* and *atter*, Anglo-Saxon for *adder*. *Cockatrice*, it seems, was but another name for the *basilisk*. So in Browne's *Vulgar Errors*, Book iii. chap. 7: "Many opinions are passant concerning the *basilisk*, or little king of serpents, commonly called the *cockatrice*." And again: "As for the generation of the *basilisk*, that it proceedeth from a *cock's egg*, hatched under a toad or serpent, it is a conceit as monstrous as the brood itself." See page 59, note 15.

[5] She seems to allude to the ancient mode of punishing a regicide, or other criminals, by placing a crown of iron heated red-hot upon his head. In some of the monkish accounts of a place of future torments, a *burning crown* is likewise appropriated to those who deprived any lawful monarch of his kingdom. The Earl of Athol, who was executed for the murder of James I., King of Scots, was previous to death crowned with a hot iron.

Anointed let me be with deadly venom;
And die, ere men can say, *God save the Queen!*

Q. Eliz. Go, go, poor soul, I envy not thy glory;
To feed my humour, wish thyself no harm.

Anne. No! why? When he that is my husband now
Came to me, as I follow'd Henry's corse;
When scarce the blood was well wash'd from his hands
Which issued from my other angel husband,
And that dead saint which then I weeping follow'd;
O, when, I say, I look'd on Richard's face,
This was my wish: *Be thou,* quoth I, *accursed,*
For making me, so young, so old a widow!
And, when thou wedd'st, let sorrow haunt thy bed;
And be thy wife — if any be so mad —
More miserable by the life of thee
Than thou hast made me by my dear lord's death!
Lo, ere I can repeat this curse again,
Even in so short a space, my woman's heart
Grossly grew captive to his honey words,
And proved the subject of mine own soul's curse,
Which ever since hath kept mine eyes from rest;
For never yet one hour in his bed
Have I enjoy'd the golden dew of sleep,
But have been wakèd by his timorous dreams.[6]
Besides, he hates me for my father Warwick;
And will, no doubt, shortly be rid of me.

---

[6] This is from the History: "He tooke ill rest a nights, laie long waking and musing, sore wearied with care and watch, rather slumbered than slept, *troubled with fearfull dreames*, suddenlie sometime start up, lept out of his bed, and ran about the chamber; so was his restless heart continuallie tossed and tumbled with the tedious impression and stormie remembrance of his abhominable deed."

Q. Eliz. Poor heart, adieu! I pity thy complaining.

Anne. No more than from my soul I mourn for yours.

Q. Eliz. Farewell, thou woeful welcomer of glory!

Anne. Adieu, poor soul, that takest thy leave of it!

Duch. [*To* DORSET.] Go thou to Richmond, and good
   fortune guide thee! —

[*To* ANNE.] Go thou to Richard, and good angels tend
   thee! —

[*To* ELIZABETH.] Go thou to sanctuary, and good thoughts
   possess thee! —

I to my grave, where peace and rest lie with me!

Eighty odd years[7] of sorrow have I seen,

And each hour's joy wreck'd with a week of teen.[8]

Q. Eliz. Stay yet, look back with me unto the Tower. —

Pity, you ancient stones, those tender babes,

Whom envy hath immured within your walls!

Rough cradle for such little pretty ones!

Rude ragged nurse, old sullen playfellow

For tender princes, use my babies well!

So foolish sorrow bids your stones farewell.   [*Exeunt.*

---

[7] Shakespeare seems here to have spoken at random. The present scene is in 1483. Richard Duke of York, the husband of this lady, had he been then living, would have been but *seventy-three* years old, and we may reasonably suppose she was not older: nor did she go speedily to the grave; she lived till 1495.

[8] *Teen* seems to have been rather a favourite word with the Poet for *grief* or *sorrow.* See *The Tempest*, page 51, note 15.

SCENE II.—*The Same.   A Room of State in the Palace.*

Sennet.   Enter RICHARD, *crowned;* BUCKINGHAM, CATESBY,
a Page, *and others.*

K. Rich. Stand all apart.—Cousin of Buckingham,—

Buck. My gracious sovereign?

K. Rich. Give me thy hand. [*Ascends the throne.*] Thus
    high, by thy advice
And thy assistance, is King Richard seated:
But shall we wear these honours for a day?
Or shall they last, and we rejoice in them?

Buck. Still live they, and for ever let them last!

K. Rich. Ah, Buckingham, now do I play the touch,[1]
To try if thou be current gold indeed:
Young Edward lives; think now what I would speak.

Buck. Say on, my loving lord.

K. Rich. Why, Buckingham, I say, I would be king.

Buck. Why, so you are, my thrice-renownèd liege.

K. Rich. Ha! am I king? 'tis so: but Edward lives.

Buck. True, noble prince.

K. Rich.   O bitter consequence,
That Edward still should live! *True, noble prince!*—
Cousin, thou wert not wont to be so dull:
Shall I be plain? I wish the bastards dead;
And I would have it suddenly perform'd.
What say'st thou now? speak suddenly,[2] be brief.

Buck. Your Grace may do your pleasure.

K. Rich. Tut, tut, thou art all ice, thy kindness freezes:

---

1 To *play the touch* is to do the office of the *touchstone,* that is, a test, to
prove the quality of a thing.

2 *Suddenly* is here the same as *quickly.*

Say, have I thy consent that they shall die?

Buck. Give me some breath, some little pause, my lord,
Before I positively speak herein :
I will resolve[3] your Grace immediately.   [*Exit.*

 Cate. [*Aside to another.*] The King is angry; see, he
  gnaws his lip.

 K. Rich. I will converse with iron-witted fools
And unrespective boys :[4]   [*Descends from his throne.*
     none are for me
That look into me with considerate eyes :
High-reaching Buckingham grows circumspect. —
Boy ! —

 Page. My lord?

 K. Rich. Know'st thou not any whom corrupting gold
Would tempt unto a close exploit of death?

 Page. I know a discontented gentleman,
Whose humble means match not his haughty mind :
Gold were as good as twenty orators,
And will, no doubt, tempt him to any thing.

 K. Rich. What is his name?

 Page.   His name, my lord, is Tyrrel.

 K. Rich. I partly know the man : go call him hither. —
          [*Exit* Page.
The deep-revolving witty[5] Buckingham
No more shall be the neighbour to my counsels :
Hath he so long held out with me untired,
And stops he now for breath? well, be it so. —

---

 [3] *Resolve* in the sense of *inform* or *satisfy;* a frequent usage.

 [4] *Unrespective* is *inconsiderate* or *unthoughtful;* in accordance with the
old use of *respect.* See page 140, note 20.

 [5] *Witty* was employed to signify a *man of sagacity, wisdom,* or *judgment;*
or, as Baret defines it, " *having the senses sharp, perceiving or foreseeing
quicklie.*"

Enter STANLEY.

How now! what news with you?

Stan. My lord, I hear the Marquess Dorset's fled
To Richmond, in those parts beyond the seas
Where he abides.

K. Rich. Come hither, Catesby: rumour it abroad
That Anne, my wife, is very grievous sick;
I will take order for her keeping close.
Inquire me out some mean-born gentleman,
Whom I will marry straight to Clarence' daughter;
The boy is foolish,[6] and I fear not him.
Look, how thou dream'st! I say again, give out
That Anne my Queen is sick, and like to die:
About it; for it stands me much upon,[7]
To stop all hopes whose growth may damage me. —

[*Exit* CATESBY.

I must be married to my brother's daughter,
Or else my kingdom stands on brittle glass:
Murder her brothers, and then marry her!
Uncertain way of gain! But I am in
So far in blood, that sin will pluck on sin:
Tear-falling pity dwells not in this eye. —

Re-enter the Page, *with* TYRREL.

[6] This youth, who is known in history as Edward Earl of Warwick, was at that time but about ten years old. He was put to death by Henry VII. in 1499; he being then the only surviving male of the Plantagenet name. The chroniclers represent him as little better than an idiot; but his stupidity was most likely the result of cruel treatment; he being confined immediately after the battle of Bosworth, and his education totally neglected. It was the interest of the reigning powers to make him "foolish," or at least to have him thought so.

[7] This is an old idiomatic phrase for *it behoves me*, or, as we should now say, *it stands me in hand*. See *King Richard II.*, page 94, note 14.

Is thy name Tyrrel?

   Tyr. James Tyrrel, and your most obedient subject.

   K. Rich. Art thou indeed?

   Tyr.   Prove me, my gracious sovereign.

   K. Rich. Darest thou resolve to kill a friend of mine?

   Tyr. Ay, my lord;

But I had rather kill two enemies.

   K. Rich. Why, then thou hast it: two deep enemies,

Foes to my rest and my sweet sleep's disturbers,

Are they that I would have thee deal upon:

Tyrrel, I mean those bastards in the Tower.

   Tyr. Let me have open means to come to them,

And soon I'll rid you from the fear of them.

   K. Rich. Thou sing'st sweet music. Hark, come hither,

       Tyrrel:

Go, by this token: rise, and lend thine ear: [*Whispers.*

There is no more but so: say it is done,

And I will love thee, and prefer thee for it.

   Tyr. I will dispatch it straight.   [*Exit.*

Re-enter BUCKINGHAM.

   Buck. My lord, I have consider'd in my mind

The late demand that you did sound me in.

   K. Rich. Well, let that rest. Dorset is fled to Richmond.

   Buck. I hear the news, my lord.

   K. Rich. Stanley, he is your wife's son: well, look to it.

   Buck. My lord, I claim the gift, my due by promise,

For which your honour and your faith is pawn'd;

Th' earldom of Hereford, and the movables,

The which you promisèd I should possess.

   K. Rich. Stanley, look to your wife: if she convey

Letters to Richmond, you shall answer it.

Buck. What says your Highness to my just request?

K. Rich. I do remember me, Henry the Sixth
Did prophesy that Richmond should be king,
When Richmond was a little peevish boy.
A king! — perhaps —

Buck. My lord, —

K. Rich. How chance the prophet could not at that time
Have told me, I being by, that I should kill him?

Buck. My lord, your promise for the earldom, —

K. Rich. Richmond! When last I was at Exeter,
The mayor in courtesy show'd me the castle,
And call'd it Rouge-mont: at which name I started,
Because a bard of Ireland told me once,
I should not live long after I saw Richmond.

Buck. My lord, —

K. Rich. Ay, what's o'clock?

Buck. I am thus bold to put your Grace in mind
Of what you promised me.

K. Rich.   Well, but what's o'clock?

Buck. Upon the stroke of ten.

K. Rich.   Well, let it strike.

Buck. Why let it strike?

K. Rich. Because that, like a Jack,[8] thou keep'st the stroke
Betwixt thy begging and my meditation.
I am not in the giving vein to-day.

---

[8] This alludes to the *Jack of the clock*, which was a figure made in old
clocks to strike the bell on the outside. Richard compares Buckingham to
one of the automatons, and bids him not to suspend the stroke on the
clock bell, but strike, that the noise may be past, and himself at liberty to
pursue his meditations. The following passage from Cotgrave will further
elucidate its meaning: "A *jacke of the clocke-house*; a little busie-body,
medler, *jack-stickler*; one that has an oare in every man's boat, or his hand
in every man's dish."

Buck. Why, then resolve me whether you will or no.

K. Rich. Thou troublest me; I am not in the vein.

          [Exeunt all but BUCKINGHAM.

Buck. Is it even so? rewards he my true service
With such contempt? made I him king for this?
O, let me think on Hastings, and be gone
To Brecknock,[9] while my fearful head is on !   *[Exit.*

SCENE III. — *Another Room in the Palace.*

Enter TYRREL.

Tyr. The tyrannous and bloody act is done,
The most arch deed of piteous massacre
That ever yet this land was guilty of.
Dighton and Forrest, whom I did suborn
To do this ruthless piece of butchery,
Albeit they were flesh'd[1] villains, bloody dogs,
Melting with tenderness and mild compassion,
Wept like two children in their death's sad story.
O, thus, quoth Dighton, *lay the gentle babes,* —
Thus, thus, quoth Forrest, *girdling one another
Within their innocent alabaster arms :
Their lips were four red roses on a stalk,
Which in their summer beauty kiss'd each other.
A book of prayers on their pillow lay;*

 9 *Brecknock* was the name of Buckingham's castle in Wales.

 1 The verb to *flesh* is defined by Richardson "to train, to inure, to in-
dulge, to glut or satiate." So in *Henry V.*, iii. 1: "And the *flesh'd* soldier,
rough and hard of heart," &c. Also in Drayton's *Miseries of Queen
Margaret :*

   Both which were *flesht* abundantly with blood
   In those three battles they had won before.

Which once, quoth Forrest, *almost changed my mind;*
But, O, the Devil — there the villain stopp'd;
When Dighton thus told on : *We smotheréd*
The most replenishéd sweet work of Nature,
That from the prime creation e'er she framed.
Hence both are gone with conscience and remorse,[2]
They could not speak ; and so I left them both,
To bear this tidings to the bloody King :
And here he comes. —

Enter King RICHARD.

                All health, my sovereign lord !
  K. Rich. Kind Tyrrel, am I happy in thy news?
  Tyr. If to have done the thing you gave in charge
Beget your happiness, be happy then,
For it is done.
  K. Rich.   But didst thou see them dead?
  Tyr. I did, my lord.
  K. Rich.   And buried, gentle Tyrrel?
  Tyr. The chaplain of the Tower hath buried them ;
But where, to say the truth, I do not know.
  K. Rich. Come to me, Tyrrel, soon at[3] after supper,
When thou shalt tell the process of their death.
Meantime, but think how I may do thee good,
And be inheritor of thy desire.
Farewell till then.
  Tyr.   I humbly take my leave.   [*Exit.*
  K. Rich. The son of Clarence have I pent up close ;

---

  [2] "Conscience and remorse" probably means what we call remorse of conscience, or, simply, remorse.

  [3] Shakespeare has the phrase *soon at* several times in the sense of *about.* See *The Merchant,* page 114, note 1.

His daughter meanly have I match'd in marriage ; [4]
The sons of Edward sleep in Abraham's bosom,
And Anne my wife hath bid the world good night.
Now, for I know the Bretagne [5] Richmond aims
At young Elizabeth, my brother's daughter,
And, by that knot, looks proudly on the crown,
To her go I, a jolly thriving wooer.

Enter CATESBY.

Cate. My lord, —

K. Rich. Good news or bad, that thou comest in so
    bluntly?

Cate. Bad news, my lord : Ely is fled to Richmond ;
And Buckingham, back'd with the hardy Welshmen,
Is in the field, and still his power increaseth.

K. Rich. Ely with Richmond troubles me more near
Than Buckingham and his rash-levied strength.
Come, I have learn'd that fearful commenting
Is leaden servitor to dull delay ; [6]
Delay leads impotent and snail-paced beggary :
Then fiery expedition be my wing,

---

[4] The daughter of Clarence was in fact married to Sir Richard Pole, and
hence became the mother of Cardinal Pole. Sir Richard was half-brother
to the Countess of Richmond.

[5] He thus denominates Richmond, because after the battle of Tewksbury
he had taken refuge in the Court of Francis II., Duke of Bretagne, where
by the procurement of Edward IV. he was kept a long time in honourable
custody.

[6] *Fearful commenting* is timorous or cowardly reflection or deliberation ;
leaden of course is heavy or sluggish ; *servitor* is an old form for *servant ;*
used whenever a trisyllable is wanted with that meaning ; and *delay* is put
for *procrastination* or reluctance to act. So that the sense is, cowardly deliberation is the tardy, lingering slave of a procrastinating spirit or master.
The meaning of the next line is, that procrastination leads on to or super-
induces feeble and creeping or slow-footed beggary.

Jove's Mercury, and herald for a king ! [7]
Go, muster men : my counsel is my shield ; [8]
We must be brief, when traitors brave the field. [9]   [*Exeunt.*

SCENE IV. — *The Same. Before the Palace.*

Enter Queen MARGARET.

Q. Mar. So, now prosperity begins to mellow,
And drop into the rotten mouth of death.
Here in these confines slily have I lurk'd,
To watch the waning of mine enemies.
A dire induction [1] am I witness to,
And will to France ; hoping the consequence
Will prove as bitter, black, and tragical.
Withdraw thee, wretched Margaret : who comes here?
    [*Retires.*

Enter Queen ELIZABETH *and the Duchess of* YORK.

Q. Eliz. Ah, my poor Princes ! ah, my tender babes !
My unblown flowers, new-appearing sweets !
If yet your gentle souls fly in the air,
And be not fix'd in doom perpetual,
Hover about me with your airy wings,

---

[7] " Let my action be winged with the speed of lightning." Mercury was the old god of dispatch, and so was Jupiter's expressman. The text is made somewhat obscure by the omission of the relative ; the sense being "expedition *who is* Jove's Mercury, and *so is* a king's *proper* herald."

[8] " My shield is my counsel, and shall deliberate the matter for me." He means that he is going to discuss or debate the issue not with words, but with knocks.

[9] To " brave the field " is, probably, to *challenge, dare,* or *defy* one *to* the field or to battle. — *Brief,* again, for *quick* or *speedy.*

[1] *Induction* here is *prologue* or *preparation.* See page 47, note 7.

And hear your mother's lamentation !

    Q. Mar. [*Aside.*] Hover about her; say, that right for
        right
Hath dimm'd your infant morn to agèd night.[2]

    Duch. So many miseries have crazed my voice,
That my woe-wearied tongue is still and mute.—
Edward Plantagenet, why art thou dead?

    Q. Mar. [*Aside.*] Plantagenet doth quit[3] Plantagenet,
Edward for Edward pays a dying debt.

    Q. Eliz. Wilt Thou, O God, fly from such gentle lambs,
And throw them in the entrails of the wolf?
When didst Thou sleep while such a deed was done?

    Q. Mar. [*Aside.*] When holy Harry died, and my sweet
        son.

    Duch. Dead life, blind sight, poor mortal living ghost,
Woe's scene, world's shame, grave's due by life usurp'd,
Brief abstract and recórd of tedious days,
Rest thy unrest on England's lawful earth,[4]   [*Sitting down.*
Unlawfully made drunk with innocent blood !

    Q. Eliz. Ah, that thou wouldst as soon afford a grave
As thou canst yield a melancholy seat !

---

   [2] Meaning, apparently, that the Divine Justice, which was alleged in i. 3,
as having righted others against her, and avenged the death of Rutland by
that of her son Edward, is now turning upon her side, and righting her
against others.

   [3] To *quit* was often used for to *acquit*, and also for to *requite.* Here it
may have either sense; perhaps it has both senses. Margaret may regard
the death of her Edward as having been *avenged* by that of the other
Edward; or she may think of the latter as offsetting, or atoning for, the
former: so that the requital may itself serve for an acquittal. — To " pay a
dying debt " is, I suppose, to pay a debt by dying.

   [4] It is not very apparent why, or in what sense, *lawful* is here used:
perhaps merely for a verbal antithesis to *unlawful.* Or is the speaker regarding England as the proper seat of order and law?

Then would I hide my bones, not rest them here.

Ah, who hath any cause to mourn but I?

                                [Sitting down by her.

    Q. Mar. *[Coming forward.]* If ancient sorrow be most
       reverend,

Give mine the benefit of seniory,[5]

And let my griefs frown on the upper hand.

If sorrow can admit society,   *[Sitting down with them.*

Tell o'er your woes again by viewing mine :

I had an Edward, till a Richard kill'd him ;

I had a Harry, till a Richard kill'd him :

Thou hadst an Edward, till a Richard kill'd him ;

Thou hadst a Richard, till a Richard kill'd him.

    Duch. I had a Richard too, and thou didst kill him ;

I had a Rutland too, thou holp'st to kill him.

    Q. Mar. Thou hadst a Clarence too, and Richard kill'd
       him.

From forth the kennel of thy womb hath crept

A hell-hound that doth hunt us all to death :

That dog, that had his teeth before his eyes,[6]

To worry lambs, and lap their gentle blood ;

That foul defacer of God's handiwork ;

That excellent-grand tyrant of the Earth,

---

    [5] *Seniory* is but a shortened form of *seniority.* — *Ancient* here has the sense of *aged* or *veteran.* Margaret's sorrow is *older* than that of the others. — To " frown on the upper hand " is to have precedence in the right of expression.

    [6] Alluding to the tradition that Richard, at his birth, had his mouth armed with teeth. So, in v. 6, of the preceding play, Richard says in reference to his birth,

           The midwife wonder'd, and the women cried,
           O, Jesus bless us, he is born with teeth !
           And so I was; which plainly signified
           That I should snarl, and bite, and play the dog.

That reigns in gallèd eyes[7] of weeping souls ;
Thy womb let loose, to chase us to our graves. —
O upright, just, and true-disposing God,
How do I thank Thee, that this carnal[8] cur
Preys on the issue of his mother's body,
And makes her pew-fellow[9] with others' moan !

Duch. O Harry's wife, triúmph not in my woes !
God witness with me, I have wept for thine.

Q. Mar. Bear with me ; I am hungry for revenge,
And now I cloy me with beholding it.
Thy Edward he is dead, that kill'd my Edward ;
Thy other Edward dead, to quit my Edward ;
Young York he is but boot,[10] because both they
Match not the high perfection of my loss :
Thy Clarence he is dead that stabb'd my Edward ;
And the beholders of this tragic play,
Th' adulterate[11] Hastings, Rivers, Vaughan, Grey,
Untimely smother'd in their dusky graves.
Richard yet lives, Hell's black intelligencer ;
Only reserved their[12] factor, to buy souls,
And send them thither : but at hand, at hand,

---

[7] **Eyes** inflamed with weeping, or made red with " eye-offending brine."
So in *Hamlet*, i. 2 : " The salt of most unrighteous tears had left the flush-
ing in her gallèd eyes."

[8] *Carnal* for *sanguinary* or *blood-thirsty* ; as in *Hamlet*, v. 2 : " So shall
you hear of *carnal*, bloody, and unnatural acts."

[9] *Pew-fellow* is *companion* or *participator*. The Poet has *coach-fellow* in
the same sense, apparently.

[10] *Boot* is an old word for any thing thrown into a bargain.

[11] *Adulterate* is *stained with adultery*. Alluding to Jane Shore.

[12] *Their* refers to *Hell*, which is used as a collective noun. — *Intelligencer*
sometimes has the sense of *intelligencing* or *giving intelligence*. Here it
seems to mean *spokesman*, *mouth-piece*, or *organ of communication*. — Of
course *factor* is *agent*.

Ensues his piteous and unpitied end :
Earth gapes, Hell burns, fiends roar, saints pray,
To have him suddenly convey'd from hence. —
Cancel his bond of life,[13] dear God, I pray,
That I may live to say, *The dog is dead !*

    Q. Eliz. O, thou didst prophesy the time would come
That I should wish for thee to help me curse
That bottled spider, that foul bunch-back'd toad !

    Q. Mar. I call'd thee then vain flourish of my fortune ;
I call'd thee then poor shadow, painted queen ;
The presentation of but what I was ;
The flattering index of a direful pageant ;[14]
One heaved a-high, to be hurl'd down below ;
A mother only mock'd with two sweet babes ;
A dream of what thou wert ; a breath, a bubble ;
A sign of dignity, a garish flag
To be the aim of every dangerous shot ;[15]
A queen in jest, only to fill the scene.
Where is thy husband now ? where be thy brothers ?
Where be thy two sons ? wherein dost thou joy ?
Who sues to thee, and cries, *God save the Queen ?*
Where be the bending peers that flatter'd thee ?
Where be the thronging troops that follow'd thee ?
Decline all this [16] and see what now thou art :
For happy wife, a most distressèd widow ;

---

    [13] The image is of a deed or indenture securing a life-tenure of property. So in *Macbeth*, iii. 2 : "*Cancel* and tear to pieces that great *bond* which keeps me paled."

    [14] The *index* of a pageant was probably a painted cloth hung up before a booth where a pageant was to be exhibited. See page 101, note 17.

    [15] Alluding to the dangerous situation of those persons to whose care the standards of armies were intrusted.

    [16] That is, run it through all the moods and tenses.

For joyful mother, one that wails the name ;
For queen, a very caitiff crown'd with care ;
For one being sued-to, one that humbly sues ;
For one commanding all, obey'd of none ;
For one that scorn'd at me, now scorn'd of me :
Thus hath the course of justice wheel'd about,
And left thee but a very prey to time ;
Having no more but thought of what thou wert,
To torture thee the more, being what thou art.
Thou didst usurp my place, and dost thou not
Usurp the just proportion of my sorrow?
Now thy proud neck bears half my burden'd yoke ;
From which even here I slip my wearied head,
And leave the burden of it all on thee.
Farewell, York's wife ; and queen of sad mischance :
These English woes will make me smile in France.

   Q. Eliz. O thou well-skill'd in curses, stay awhile,
And teach me how to curse mine enemies !

   Q. Mar. Forbear to sleep the night, and fast the day ;
Compare dead happiness with living woe ;
Think that thy babes were fairer than they were,
And he that slew them fouler than he is :
Bettering[17] thy loss makes the bad-causer worse :
Revolving this will teach thee how to curse.

   Q. Eliz. My words are dull ; O, quicken them with
       thine !

   Q. Mar. Thy woes will make them sharp, and pierce like
       mine.   [*Exit.*

   Duch. Why should calamity be full of words?

---

[17] *Bettering* is here used in the sense of *exaggerating* or *magnifying*
"The greater you conceive your loss to be, the worse the author of it will
seem."

Q. Eliz. Windy attorneys [18] to their client woes,
Airy succeeders of intestate joys, [19]
Poor breathing orators of miseries !
Let them have scope : though what they do impart
Help nothing else, yet do they ease the heart. [20]

Duch. If so, then be not tongue-tied : go with me,
And in the breath of bitter words let's smother
My damnèd son, that thy two sweet sons smother'd.

[*Drum within.*

I hear his drum : be copious in exclaims.

Enter King RICHARD *and his Train, marching.*

K. Rich. Who intercepts me in my expedition ?
Duch. O, she that might have intercepted thee,
By strangling thee in her accursèd womb,
From all the slaughters, wretch, that thou hast done !

Q. Eliz. Hidest thou that forehead with a golden crown,
Where should be branded, if that right were right,
The slaughter of the Prince that owed that crown,
And the dire death of my poor sons and brothers ?
Tell me, thou villain-slave, where are my children ?

Duch. Thou toad, thou toad, where is thy brother Clarence ?

---

[18] Words are called "*windy* attorneys," because they are made up of wind. In his *Venus and Adonis* the Poet figures the tongue as the heart's attorney :

> But when the heart's *attorney* once is mute,
> The *client* breaks, as desperate of his suit.

[19] The joys, being all consumed and passed away, have died intestate ; that is, have made no will, having nothing to bequeath ; and mere verbal complaints are their successors, but inherit nothing but misery.

[20] This seems to have been rather a favourite idea with the Poet. So in *Macbeth*, iv. 3 :

> Give sorrow words ; the grief that does not speak
> Whispers the o'erfraught heart, and bids it break.

And little Ned Plantagenet, his son?

    Q. Eliz. Where is the gentle Rivers, Vaughan, Grey?

    Duch. Where is kind Hastings?

    K. Rich. A flourish, trumpets! strike alarum, drums!
Let not the Heavens hear these tell-tale women
Rail on the Lord's anointed: strike, I say!—

                           [*Flourish. Alarum.*
Either be patient, and entreat me fair,
Or with the clamorous report of war
Thus will I drown your exclamations.

    Duch. Art thou my son?

    K. Rich. Ay, I thank God, my father, and yourself.

    Duch. Then patiently hear my impatience.

    K. Rich. Madam, I have a touch of your condition,[21]
That cannot brook the accent of reproof.

    Duch. O, let me speak!

    K. Rich.   Do, then; but I'll not hear.

    Duch. I will be mild and gentle in my words.

    K. Rich. And brief, good mother; for I am in haste.

    Duch. Art thou so hasty? I have stay'd for thee,
God knows, in torment and in agony.

    K. Rich. And came I not at last to comfort you?

    Duch. No, by the holy Rood, thou know'st it well,
Thou camest on Earth to make the Earth my hell.
A grievous burden was thy birth to me;
Tetchy and wayward was thy infancy;
Thy school-days frightful, desperate, wild, and furious;
Thy prime of manhood daring, bold, and venturous;
Thy age confirm'd, proud, subtle, bloody, treacherous,
More mild, but yet more harmful-kind in hatred:

    21 A *smack* or *spice* of your *disposition* or *temper*. For this use of *condi-
tion* see *As You Like It*, page 46, note 25.

What comfortable hour canst thou name,
That ever graced me in thy company?

    K. Rich.   Faith, none, but Humphrey Hower,[22] that call'd
       your Grace
To breakfast once forth of my company.
If I be so disgracious in your eye,
Let me march on, and not offend you, madam. —
Strike up the drum.

    Duch.   I pr'ythee, hear me speak.

    K. Rich.   You speak too bitterly.

    Duch.   Hear me a word ;
For I shall never speak to thee again.

    K. Rich.   So.

    Duch.   Either thou'lt die, by God's just ordinance,
Ere from this war thou turn a conqueror ;
Or I with grief and éxtreme age shall perish,
And never look upon thy face again.

---

[22] So printed in the old copies. No satisfactory explanation of the passage has yet been discovered. A part of St. Paul's Cathedral was called Duke Humphrey's Walk, because Humphrey, sometime Duke of Gloucester, was supposed to be buried there. As the old Cathedral was a place of great resort, those who were hard up for a dinner used to saunter there, perhaps in the hope of being asked to dinner by some of their acquaintance. Hence grew the phrase of " dining with Duke Humphrey," used of those who thus " waited upon Providence " for a chance to eat. And Steevens thinks that " Shakespeare might by this strange phrase, *Humphrey Hour*, have designed to mark the hour at which the good Duchess was as hungry as the followers of Duke Humphrey." Singer thinks " it is possible that by *Humphrey Hower* Richard alludes to the hour of his birth, the *hour* after which his mother ate out of his company." And he quotes the old vulgar saying, that a teeming woman feeds two. According to this, *Humphrey Hower* might be meant as the name of the physician who attended the Duchess when her Richard was born. Staunton " apprehends that *Humphrey Hour* was nothing more than a cant phrase for *eating-hour*." None of these explanations can hold my assent, nor can I think of any better.

Therefore take with thee my most heavy curse ;
Which, in the day of battle, tire thee more
Than all the cómplete armour that thou wear'st !
My prayers on the adverse party fight ;
And there the little souls of Edward's children
Whisper the spirits of thine enemies,
And promise them success and victory.
Bloody thou art, bloody will be thy end ;
Shame serves thy life, and doth thy death attend.   [*Exit.*

   Q. Eliz. Though far more cause, yet much less spirit to
      curse
Abides in me ; I say amen to her.   [*Going.*

   K. Rich. Stay, madam ; I must speak a word with
      you.

   Q. Eliz. I have no more sons of the royal blood
For thee to murder : for my daughters, Richard,
They shall be praying nuns, not weeping queens ;
And therefore level not to hit their lives.

   K. Rich. You have a daughter call'd Elizabeth,
Virtuous and fair, royal and gracious.

   Q. Eliz. And must she die for this? O, let her live,
And I'll corrupt her manners, stain her beauty :
Slander myself as false to Edward's bed ;
Throw over her the vale of infamy :
So she may live unscarr'd of bleeding slaughter,
I will confess she was not Edward's daughter.

   K. Rich. Wrong not her birth, she is of royal blood.

   Q. Eliz. To save her life, I'll say she is not so.

   K. Rich. Her life is safest only in her birth.

   Q. Eliz. And only in that safety died her brothers.

   K. Rich. Lo, at their births good stars were opposite.

   Q. Eliz. No, to their lives bad friends were contrary.

K. Rich. All unavoided [23] is the doom of destiny.

Q. Eliz. True, when avoided grace makes destiny :
My babes were destined to a fairer death,
If grace had bless'd thee with a fairer life.

K. Rich. You speak as if that I had slain my cousins.

Q. Eliz. Cousins, indeed ; and by their uncle cozen'd
Of comfort, kingdom, kindred, freedom, life.
Whose hand soever lanced their tender hearts,
Thy head, all indirectly,[24] gave direction :
No doubt the murderous knife was dull and blunt
Till it was whetted on thy stone-hard heart,
To revel in the entrails of my lambs.
But that still [25] use of grief makes wild grief tame,
My tongue should to thy ears not name my boys
Till that my nails were anchor'd in thine eyes ;
And I, in such a desperate bay of death,
Like a poor bark, of sails and tackling reft,
Rush all to pieces on thy rocky bosom.

K. Rich. Madam, so thrive I in my enterprise
And dangerous success of bloody wars,[26]
As I intend more good to you and yours
Than ever you and yours by me were harm'd !

Q. Eliz. What good is cover'd with the face of heaven,

---

[23] *Unavoided* for *unavoidable.* So the endings *-ed* and *-able* were often
used indiscriminately. See *Richard II.*, page 79, note 35.

[24] *Indirectly* here means *wrongfully* or *wickedly ;* probably used for a
sort of jingle with *direction.* It may be worth noting, however, that the
radical sense of *right*, as also of *direct*, is *straight ;* while that of *wrong*, as
also of *indirect*, is *crooked.*

[25] The use of *still* for *continually* is very frequent : here it is used as an
adjective with the same sense, *continual.*

[26] That is, the bloody wars that are to *follow ; success* being used in the
Latin sense of *succession* or *sequel.* See *Much Ado*, page 98, note 14.

To be discover'd, that can do me good?

    K. Rich. Th' advancement of your children, gentle lady.

    Q. Eliz. Up to some scaffold, there to lose their heads?

    K. Rich. No, to the dignity and height of honour,

The high imperial type of this Earth's glory.[27]

    Q. Eliz. Flatter my sorrows with report of it;

Tell me what state, what dignity, what honour,

Canst thou demise[28] to any child of mine?

    K. Rich. Even all I have; ay, and myself and all,

Will I withal endow a child of thine;

So in the Lethe of thy angry soul

Thou drown the sad remembrance of those wrongs

Which thou supposest I have done to thee.

    Q. Eliz. Be brief, lest that the process of thy kindness

Last longer telling than thy kindness' date.

    K. Rich. Then know, that from my soul I love thy daughter.

    Q. Eliz. My daughter's mother thinks it with her soul.

    K. Rich. What do you think?

    Q. Eliz. That thou dost love my daughter from thy soul:

So, from thy soul's love, didst thou love her brothers;

And, from my heart's love,[29] I do thank thee for it.

    K. Rich. Be not so hasty to confound my meaning:

I mean, that with my soul I love thy daughter,

And do intend to make her Queen of England.

    Q. Eliz. Well, then, who dost thou mean shall be her king?

    K. Rich. Even he that makes her queen: who else should be?

---

[27] That is, the *crown*, the emblem of royalty.

[28] To *demise* is to *grant*, from *demittere*, Latin.

[29] The Queen is quibbling between the different senses of *from;* one of which is *out of*, as when we say, "Speak the truth *from* the heart"; the other, that of separation or distance, as when Hamlet says "any thing so overdone is *from the purpose* of playing."

Q. Eliz. What, thou?

K. Rich.   Even I : what think you of it, madam?

Q. Eliz. How canst thou woo her?

K. Rich.   That would I learn of you,
As one being best acquainted with her humour.

Q. Eliz. And wilt thou learn of me?

K. Rich.   Madam, with all my heart.

Q. Eliz. Send to her, by the man that slew her brothers,
A pair of bleeding hearts ; thereon engraved
Edward and York ; then haply will she weep :
Therefore present to her—as sometime Margaret
Did to thy father, steep'd in Rutland's blood—
A handkerchief ; which, say to her, did drain
The purple sap from her sweet brothers' bodies,
And bid her dry her weeping eyes withal.
If this inducement move her not to love,
Send her a letter of thy noble deeds ;
Tell her thou madest away her uncle Clarence,
Her uncle Rivers ; ay, and, for her sake,
Madest quick conveyance with her good aunt Anne.

K. Rich. You mock me, madam ; this is not the way
To win your daughter.

Q. Eliz.   There's no other way ;
Unless thou couldst put on some other shape,
And not be Richard that hath done all this.

K. Rich. Say that I did all this for love of her?

Q. Eliz. Nay, then indeed she cannot choose but love thee,
Having bought love with such a bloody spoil.

K. Rich. Look, what is done cannot be now amended :
Men shall[30] deal unadvisedly sometimes,

---

[30] *Shall* for *will ;* the two being often used indiscriminately. — *Unadvisedly* in the old sense of *inconsiderately, rashly,* or *imprudently.* See page 77, note 25.

Which after-hours give leisure to repent.
If I did take the kingdom from your sons,
To make amends, I'll give it to your daughter.
A grandam's name is little less in love
Than is the doting title of a mother ;
They are as children but one step below,
Even of your mettle, of your very blood ;
Of all one pain, — save for a night of groans
Endured of her, for whom you bid [31] like sorrow.
Your children were vexation to your youth ;
But mine shall be a comfort to your age.
The loss you have is but a son being king,
And by that loss your daughter is made queen.
I cannot make you what amends I would,
Therefore accept such kindness as I can.
Dorset your son, that with a fearful soul
Leads discontented steps in foreign soil,
This fair alliance quickly shall call home
To high promotions and great dignity :
The King, that calls your beauteous daughter wife,
Familiarly shall call thy Dorset brother ;
Again shall you be mother to a king,
And all the ruins of distressful times
Repair'd with double riches of content.
What ! we have many goodly days to see :
The liquid drops of tears that you have shed
Shall come again, transform'd to orient pearl,
Advantaging their loan with interest
Of ten-times-double gain of happiness.

---

[31] "Endured *of* her" is the same as endured *by* her; *of* being formerly used in such cases to denote the relation of agent. — *Bid* is an old preterite form for *bided*, *suffered*, or *endured*.

Go, then, my mother, to thy daughter go;
Make bold her bashful years with your experience;
Prepare her ears to hear a wooer's tale;
Put in her tender heart th' aspiring flame
Of golden sovereignty; acquaint the Princess
With the sweet silent hours of marriage joys:
And, when this arm of mine hath chástiséd
The petty rebel, dull-brain'd Buckingham,
Bound with triumphant garlands will I come,
And lead thy daughter to a conqueror's bed;
To whom I will retail[32] my conquest won,
And she shall be sole victress, Cæsar's Cæsar.

    Q. Eliz. What were I best to say? her father's brother
Would be her lord? or shall I say, her uncle?
Or, he that slew her brothers and her uncles?
Under what title shall I woo for thee,
That God, the law, my honour, and her love,
Can make seem pleasing to her tender years?

    K. Rich. Infer fair England's peace by this alliance.

    Q. Eliz. Which she shall purchase with still-lasting war.

    K. Rich. Tell her, the King, that may command, entreats.

    Q. Eliz. That at her hands which the King's King forbids.

    K. Rich. Say, she shall be a high and mighty queen.

    Q. Eliz. To wail the title, as her mother doth.

    K. Rich. Say, I will love her everlastingly.

    Q. Eliz. But how long shall that title[33] *ever* last?

    K. Rich. Sweetly in force unto her fair life's end.

    Q. Eliz. But how long fairly shall her sweet life last?

    K. Rich. As long as Heaven and Nature lengthen it.

---

[32] *Retail*, again, for *recount* or *tell over*. See page 110, note 6.

[33] The word *title* is here used in a legal or forensic sense, for interest in an estate. So says Heath.

Q. Eliz. As long as Hell and Richard like of it.

K. Rich. Say, I, her sovereign, am her subject now.

Q. Eliz. But she, your subject, loathes such sovereignty.

K. Rich. Be eloquent in my behalf to her.

Q. Eliz. An honest tale speeds best being plainly told.

K. Rich. Then, plainly to her tell my loving tale.

Q. Eliz. Plain and not honest is too harsh a style.

K. Rich. Your reasons are too shallow and too quick.

Q. Eliz. O, no, my reasons are too deep and dead;[34]
Too deep and dead, poor infants, in their graves.

K. Rich. Harp not on that string, madam; that is past.

Q. Eliz. Harp on it still shall I till heart-strings break.

K. Rich. Now, by my George,[35] my garter, and my
crown, —

Q. Eliz. Profaned, dishonour'd, and the third usurp'd.

K. Rich. —I swear—

Q. Eliz.   By nothing; for this is no oath:
Thy George, profaned, hath lost his holy honour;
Thy garter, blemish'd, pawn'd his knightly virtue;
Thy crown, usurp'd, disgraced his kingly glory.
If something thou wouldst swear to be believed,
Swear, then, by something that thou hast not wrong'd.

K. Rich. Now, by the world, —

Q. Eliz.   'Tis full of thy foul wrongs.

K. Rich. My father's death, —

Q. Eliz.   Thy life hath that dishonour'd.

K. Rich. Then, by myself, —

---

[34] The Queen implies an equivoque on *quick*, which is used by Richard in the sense of *prompt, nimble,* or *rash;* and she plays between this sense and that of *alive.*

[35] This was a figure or image of St. George on horseback, which was worn as a badge by Knights of the Garter.

Q. Eliz.   Thyself is self-misused.

K. Rich. Why, then by God,—

Q. Eliz.   God's wrong is most of all.
If thou hadst fear'd to break an oath by Him,
The unity the King thy brother made
Had not been broken, nor my brother slain :
If thou hadst fear'd to break an oath by Him,
Th' imperial metal, circling now thy head,
Had graced the tender temples of my child ;
And both the Princes had been breathing here,
Which now, two tender bedfellows for dust,
Thy broken faith hath made a prey for worms.
What canst thou swear by now?

K. Rich.   The time to come.

Q. Eliz. That thou hast wrongèd in the time o'erpast ;
For I myself have many tears to wash
Hereafter time, for time past wrong'd by thee.
The children live, whose parents thou hast slaughter'd,
Ungovern'd youth, to wail it in their age ;
The parents live, whose children thou hast butcher'd,
Old wither'd plants, to wail it with their age.
Swear not by time to come ; for that thou hast
Misused ere used, by time misused o'erpast.

K. Rich. As I intend to prosper and repent,
So thrive I in my dangerous affairs
Of hostile arms ! myself myself confound !
Heaven and fortune bar me happy hours !
Day, yield me not thy light ; nor, night, thy rest !
Be opposite all planets of good luck
To my proceeding !—if, with pure heart's love,
Immaculate devotion, holy thoughts,
I tender not thy beauteous princely daughter !

In her consists my happiness and thine ;
Without her, follows to myself and thee,
Herself, the land, and many a Christian soul,
Death, desolation, ruin, and decay :
It cannot be avoided but by this ;
It will not be avoided but by this.
Therefore, dear mother,—I must call you so,—
Be the attorney of my love to her :
Plead what I will be, not what I have been ;
Not my deserts, but what I will deserve :
Urge the necessity and state of times,
And be not peevish-fond [36] in great designs.

 Q. Eliz. Shall I be tempted of the Devil thus?

 K. Rich. Ay, if the Devil tempt thee to do good.

 Q. Eliz. Shall I forget myself to be myself?

 K. Rich. Ay, if yourself's remembrance wrong yourself.

 Q. Eliz. Shall I go win my daughter to thy will?

 K. Rich. And be a happy mother by the deed.

 Q. Eliz. I go. — Write to me very shortly,
And you shall understand from me her mind.[37]

 K. Rich. Bear her my true love's kiss ; and so, farewell. —

    [Kissing her. Exit Queen ELIZABETH.

Relenting fool, and shallow-changing woman ! —

   Enter RATCLIFF ; CATESBY *following.*

[36] Both *fond* and *peevish* are often used by Shakespeare for *foolish.* So in scene 2 of this Act : "When Richmond was a little *peevish* boy." The compound seems to have about the same meaning as *childish-foolish*, which occurs in i. 3, of this play. Or *peevish* may here have the sense of *perverse.*

[37] This representation is in substance historical ; and some of the old chroniclers are rather hard on Elizabeth for thus yielding to Richard's persuasions. But there is good reason to think that she outwitted him, and that her consent was but feigned in order to gain time, and to save her daughter from the fate that had overtaken her sons.

How now ! what news ?

Rat. My gracious sovereign, on the western coast
Rideth a puissant navy ; to the shore
Throng many doubtful hollow-hearted friends,
Unarm'd and unresolved to beat them back :
'Tis thought that Richmond is their admiral ;
And there they hull,[38] expecting but the aid
Of Buckingham to welcome them ashore.

   K. Rich. Some light-foot friend post to the Duke of Nor-
     folk : —
Ratcliff, thyself, — or Catesby ; where is he ?

   Cate. Here, my good lord.

   K. Rich. Fly to the duke. — [*To* RATCLIFF.] Post thou
     to Salisbury :
When thou comest thither, — [*To* CATESBY.] Dull, unmind-
     ful villain,
Why stay'st thou here, and go'st not to the duke ?

   Cate. First, mighty liege, tell me your Highness' pleasure,
What from your Grace I shall deliver to him.

   K. Rich. O, true, good Catesby : bid him levy straight
The greatest strength and power he can make,
And meet me suddenly at Salisbury.

   Cate. I go.   [*Exit.*

   Rat. What, may it please you, shall I do at Salisbury ?

   K. Rich. Why, what wouldst thou do there before I go ?

   Rat. Your Highness told me I should post before.

Enter STANLEY.

---

[38] A ship is said to *hull* when she hauls in her sails, and lays-to, without
coming to anchor, and so floats hither and thither as the waves carry her. See
Twelfth Night, page 50, note 18. — *Expecting*, here, is *waiting for*. Repeatedly so.

K. Rich. My mind is changed. — Stanley, what news with
    you?

Stan. None good, my liege, to please you with the hearing;
Nor none so bad, but well may be reported.

K. Rich. Heyday, a riddle! neither good nor bad!
What need'st thou run so many miles about,
When thou mayst tell thy tale the nearest way?
Once more, what news?

Stan.   Richmond is on the seas.

K. Rich. There let him sink, and be the seas on him,
White-liver'd runagate![39] what doth he there?

Stan. I know not, mighty sovereign, but by guess.

K. Rich. Well, as you guess?

Stan. Stirr'd up by Dorset, Buckingham, and Ely,
He makes for England, here, to claim the crown.

K. Rich. Is the chair empty? is the sword unsway'd?
Is the King dead? the empire unpossess'd?
What heir of York is there alive but we?
And who is England's King but great York's heir?
Then, tell me, what makes he upon the seas?

Stan. Unless for that, my liege, I cannot guess.

K. Rich. Unless for that [40] he comes to be your liege,
You cannot guess wherefore the Welshman comes.
Thou wilt revolt, and fly to him, I fear.

Stan. No, mighty liege; therefore mistrust me not.

K. Rich. Where is thy power, then, to beat him back?

[39] *Runagate* is *runaway* or *vagabond.* *White-liver'd, lily-liver'd,* and
milk-livered are terms denoting extreme cowardice. In v. 3, Richard calls
Richmond "a milksop." Richmond had in fact escaped the fate of the
Lancastrian leaders by fleeing into France.

[40] The words *for that* are here equivalent to *because;* a common usage
with the old writers. Richard chooses to take the phrase in another sense
than Stanley had meant.

Where be thy tenants and thy followers?
Are they not now upon the western shore,
Safe-cónducting the rebels from their ships?

   Stan. No, my good lord, my friends are in the North.

   K. Rich. Cold friends to me : what do they in the North,
When they should serve their sovereign in the West?

   Stan. They have not been commanded, mighty King :
Pleaseth your Majesty to give me leave,
I'll muster up my friends, and meet your Grace
Where and what time your Majesty shall please.

   K. Rich. Ay, ay, thou wouldst be gone to join with Rich-
      mond :
I will not trust you, sir.

   Stan.   Most mighty sovereign,
You have no cause to hold my friendship doubtful :
I never was nor never will be false.

   K. Rich. Go, then, and muster men.   But leave behind
Your son, George Stanley : look your faith be firm,
Or else his head's assurance is but frail.

   Stan. So deal with him as I prove true to you.   [*Exit.*

Enter a Messenger.

   Mess. My gracious sovereign, now in Devonshire,
As I by friends am well advértiséd,[41]
Sir Edward Courtney, and the haughty prelate
Bishop of Exeter, his elder brother,
With many more confederates, are in arms.

Enter a second Messenger.

   2 Mess. In Kent, my liege, the Guildfords are in arms ;

---

[41] *Advertised* for *informed, notified,* or *instructed,* occurs repeatedly.

And every hour more competitors [42]
Flock to the rebels, and their power grows strong.

Enter a third Messenger.

3 Mess. My lord, the army of great Buckingham—
K. Rich. Out on ye, owls! nothing but songs of death? [43]
                                [Strikes him.
There, take thou that, till thou bring better news.
   3 Mess. The news I have to tell your Majesty
Is, that by sudden floods and fall of waters,
Buckingham's army is dispersed and scatter'd;
And he himself wander'd away alone,
No man knows whither.
    K. Rich.   O, I cry thee mercy:
There is my purse to cure that blow of thine.
Hath any well-advisèd friend proclaim'd
Reward to him that brings the traitor in?
   3 Mess. Such proclamation hath been made, my lord.

Enter a fourth Messenger.

   4 Mess. Sir Thomas Lovel and Lord Marquess Dorset,
'Tis said, my liege, in Yorkshire are in arms.
But this good comfort bring I to your Highness,
The Bretagne navy is dispersed by tempest:
Richmond, in Dorsetshire, sent out a boat
Unto the shore, to ask those on the banks
If they were his assistants, yea or no;
Who answer'd him, they came from Buckingham
Upon his party: [44] he, mistrusting them,

   [42] *Competitors* for *confederates* or *partners.* See *Twelfth Night,* page
114, note 3.
   [43] The owl's note or hoot was considered ominous or ill-boding.
   [44] " Upon his party" is to take part with him; to fight on his side.

Hoised sail, and made his course again for Bretagne.

   K. Rich. March on, march on, since we are up in arms ;
If not to fight with foreign enemies,
Yet to beat down these rebels here at home.

Re-enter CATESBY.

   Cate. My liege, the Duke of Buckingham is taken, —
That is the best news : that the Earl of Richmond
Is with a mighty power landed at Milford,
Is colder tidings, yet they must be told.[45]

   K. Rich. Away towards Salisbury ! while we reason here,[46]
A royal battle might be won and lost : —
Some one take order[47] Buckingham be brought
To Salisbury ; the rest march on with me. [*Flourish. Exeunt.*

SCENE V. — A Room in Lord STANLEY'S House.

Enter STANLEY and Sir CHRISTOPHER URSWICK.

   Stan. Sir Christopher, tell Richmond this from me :
That, in the sty of the most bloody boar,
My son George Stanley is frank'd up in hold :
If I revolt, off goes young George's head ;
The fear of that holds off my present aid.
But, tell me, where is princely Richmond now?

---

[45] The Earl of Richmond embarked with about two thousand men at Harfleur, in Normandy, August 1, 1485, and landed at Milford Haven on the 7th. He directed his course to Wales, hoping the Welsh would receive him cordially as their countryman, he having been born at Pembroke, and his grandfather being Owen Tudor, who married Catharine of France, the widow of Henry the Fifth and mother of Henry the Sixth.

[46] That is, "while we *are talking* here." See page 103, note 4.

[47] To *take order* is, in old English, to adopt measures, or give directions.

Chris. At Pembroke, or at Ha'rford-West,[1] in Wales.

Stan. What men of name resort to him?

Chris. Sir Walter Herbert, a renownèd soldier;
Sir Gilbert Talbot, Sir William Stanley;
Oxford, redoubted Pembroke, Sir James Blunt,
And Rice ap Thomas, with a valiant crew;
And many more of noble fame and worth:
And towards London they do bend[2] their course
If by the way they be not fought withal.

Stan. Return unto thy lord; commend me to him:
Tell him the Queen hath heartily consented
He shall espouse Elizabeth her daughter.
These letters will resolve[3] him of my mind.   [*Giving letters.*
Farewell.   [*Exeunt.*

ACT V.

Scene I. — *Salisbury.   An open Place.*

Enter the Sheriff, *and* Guard, *with* Buckingham, *led to Execution.*

Buck. Will not King Richard let me speak with him?

Sher. No, my good lord; therefore be patient.

Buck. Hastings, and Edward's children, Rivers, Grey,
Holy King Henry, and thy fair son Edward,
Vaughan, and all that have miscarriéd
By underhand corrupted foul injustice, —

---

[1] This name in full is *Haverford*-West; shortened for metre's sake, of course.   The place lies nearly north of Pembroke.

[2] To *bend* occurs often in the sense of to *direct*.

[3] *Resolve*, again, for *inform* or *satisfy*.   See page 149, note 3.

If that your moody discontented souls
Do through the clouds behold this present hour,
Even for revenge mock my destruction ! —
This is All-Souls' day, fellows, is it not?

Sher. It is, my lord.

Buck. Why, then All-Souls' day [1] is my body's doomsday.
This is the day that, in King Edward's time,
I wish'd might fall on me, when I was found
False to his children or his wife's allies ;
This is the day wherein I wish'd to fall
By the false faith of him I trusted most ;
This, this All-Souls' day to my fearful soul
Is the determined respite of my wrongs : [2]
That high All-seer that I dallied with
Hath turn'd my feignèd prayer on my head,
And given in earnest what I begg'd in jest.
Thus doth He force the swords of wicked men
To turn their own points on their masters' bosoms :
Thus Margaret's curse falls heavy on my neck :
When he, quoth she, *shall split thy heart with sorrow,*
Remember Margaret was a prophetess. —
Come, sirs, convey me to the block of shame ;
Wrong hath but wrong, and blame the due of blame.

[*Exeunt.*

---

[1] Buckingham was executed on All-Saints' day, November 1, 1483.

[2] That is, " the *close* or *termination* of the period for which the punishment of my *crimes* was *deferred.*

SCENE II. — *Plain near Tamworth.*

Enter, with drum and colours, RICHMOND,[3] OXFORD,[4] *Sir*
　JAMES BLUNT, *Sir* WALTER HERBERT, *and others, with*
　Forces, marching.

Richm.　Fellows in arms, and my most loving friends,
Bruised underneath the yoke of tyranny,
Thus far into the bowels of the land
Have we march'd on without impediment;
And here receive we from our father Stanley
Lines of fair comfort and encouragement.
The wretched, bloody, and usurping boar,
That spoils your summer fields and fruitful vines,
Swills your warm blood like wash, and makes his trough
In your embowell'd bosoms, — this foul swine
Lies now even in the centre of this isle,
Near to the town of Leicester, as we learn:
From Tamworth thither is but one day's march.
In God's name, cheerly on, courageous friends,
To reap the harvest of perpetual peace
By this one bloody trial of sharp war.

[3] It has already been noted that on his father's side the Earl of Richmond was grandson to Owen Tudor. His mother was Margaret, daughter and heir to John Beaufort, the first Duke of Somerset, and great-granddaughter to John of Ghent by Catharine Swynford; on which account, after the death of Henry VI. and his son, Richmond was looked to by both friends and foes as the next male representative of the Lancastrian line. The Lancastrians all regarded him as their natural chief; and many of the Yorkists accepted him because of his having bound himself by solemn oath to marry the Princess Elizabeth, whom they of course considered the rightful heir to the crown after the death of her brothers.

[4] This Earl of Oxford was John de Vere, whose character, together with that of his son Arthur, is so finely delineated in Scott's *Anne of Geierstein.*

Oxf. Every man's conscience is a thousand swords,
To fight against this guilty homicide.

Herb. I doubt not but his friends will turn to us.

Blunt. He hath no friends but what are friends for fear,
Which in his dearest need will shrink from him.

Richm. All for our vantage. Then, in God's name,
    march :
True hope is swift, and flies with swallow's wings ;
Kings it makes gods, and meaner creatures kings. [*Exeunt.*

SCENE III. — *Bosworth Field.*

Enter King RICHARD *and Forces, the Duke of* NORFOLK,
Earl of SURREY, *and others.*

K. Rich. Here pitch our tents, even here in Bosworth
    field. —
My Lord of Surrey, why look you so sad?

Sur. My heart is ten times lighter than my looks.

K. Rich. My Lord of Norfolk, —

Nor.   Here, most gracious liege.

K. Rich. Norfolk, we must have knocks ; ha ! must we
    not?

Nor. We must both give and take, my loving lord.

K. Rich. Up with my tent ! here will I lie to-night ;
                [*Soldiers begin to set up his tent.*
But where to-morrow? Well, all's one for that. —
Who hath descried the number of the traitors?

Nor. Six or seven thousand is their utmost power.

K. Rich. Why, our battalia trebles that account : [1]

---

[1] Richmond's forces are said to have been only five thousand; and
Richard's army consisted of about twelve thousand. But Lord Stanley lay

Besides, the King's name is a tower of strength,
Which they upon the adverse party want. —
Up with the tent! — Come, noble gentlemen,
Let us survey the vantage of the ground;
Call for some men of sound direction: [2]
Let's lack no discipline, make no delay;
For, lords, to-morrow is a busy day.   [*Exeunt.*

Enter, on the other side of the field, RICHMOND, *Sir* WILLIAM
    BRANDON, OXFORD, *and others. Some of the* Soldiers
    pitch RICHMOND'S *tent.*

  Richm. The weary Sun hath made a golden set,
And, by the bright track of his fiery car,
Gives token of a goodly day to-morrow. —
Sir William Brandon, you shall bear my standard. —
Give me some ink and paper in my tent:
I'll draw the form and model of our battle,
Limit [3] each leader to his several charge,
And part in just proportion our small power. —
My Lord of Oxford, — you, Sir William Brandon, —
And you, Sir Walter Herbert, — stay with me. —
The Earl of Pembroke keeps his regiment: [4] —

---

at a small distance with three thousand men; and Richard may be supposed to have reckoned on them as his friends, though the event proved
otherwise.

  [2] Men of tried judgment and approved military skill.

  [3] That is, *direct* or *appoint* the leaders what part they are *separately* to
perform in the forthcoming conflict. The Poet has to *limit* repeatedly so.
See page 121, note 1.

  [4] "*Keeps* his *regiment*" is, in our phrase, *remains with* his *command;
regiment* being used, not for the regimental portion of an army, but in the
old sense of *government*. So, in the next speech, it is said that Lord Stanley's "regiment lies half a mile at least south from the mighty power of the
King. — *Keep* is repeatedly used by the Poet for *dwell* or *stay*.

Good Captain Blunt, bear my good-night to him,
And by the second hour in the morning
Desire the earl to see me in my tent:
Yet one thing more, good captain, do for me,—
Where is Lord Stanley quarter'd,[5] do you know?

 Blunt. Unless I have mista'en his colours much,—
Which well I am assured I have not done,—
His regiment lies half a mile at least
South from the mighty power of the King.

 Richm. If without peril it be possible,
Sweet Blunt, make some good means to speak with him,
And give him from me this most needful note.

 Blunt. Upon my life, my lord, I'll undertake it;
And so, God give you quiet rest to-night!

 Richm. Good night, good Captain Blunt. [*Exit* BLUNT.]
   —Come, gentlemen,
Let us consult upon to-morrow's business:
In to my tent; the air is raw and cold.

       [*They withdraw into the tent.*

Re-enter, to his tent, King RICHARD, NORFOLK, RATCLIFF,
    CATESBY, *and others.*

 K. Rich. What is't o'clock?

 Cate.   It's supper-time, my lord;
It's nine o'clock.

 K. Rich. I will not sup to-night.—
What, is my beaver easier than it was?[6]

---

[5] To *quarter* is still in use as a military term for to *lodge* or *encamp*.

[6] The *beaver* was a part of the helmet fixed on a sort of hinge at the ear, so as to be drawn down over the face or pushed up over the forehead, as the wearer chose or had occasion. It is probably in reference to this motion that *easier* is used of it.

And all my armour laid into my tent?

Cate. It is, my liege ; and all things are in readiness.

K. Rich. Good Norfolk, hie thee to thy charge ;
Use careful watch, choose trusty sentinels.

Nor. I go, my lord.

K. Rich. Stir with the lark to-morrow, gentle Norfolk.

Nor. I warrant you, my lord.   [*Exit.*

K. Rich. Catesby, —

Cate. My lord?

K. Rich.   Send out a pursuivant-at-arms
To Stanley's regiment ; bid him bring his power
Before sunrising, lest his son George fall
Into the blind cave of eternal night. —   [*Exit* CATESBY.
Fill me a bowl of wine. — Give me a watch.[7] —
Saddle white Surrey for the field to-morrow. —
Look that my staves[8] be sound, and not too heavy. —
Ratcliff, —

Rat. My lord?

K. Rich. Saw'st thou the melancholy Lord Northumberland?

Rat. Thomas the Earl of Surrey, and himself,
Much about cock-shut time,[9] from troop to troop

---

[7] In calling for a *watch* Richard evidently does not mean a *sentinel ;* for that guard should be kept about his tent was a matter of course. The *watch* called for is, no doubt, a *watch-light*, which was a night-candle so marked as to indicate how long it had burned, and thus serve the purpose of a modern *watch*.

[8] That is, the *staves* or poles of his lances. It was the custom to carry more than one into the field.

[9] A *cock-shut* was a large net stretched across a glade, and so suspended upon poles as easily to be drawn together, and was employed to catch woodcocks. These nets were chiefly used in the twilight of the evening, when woodcocks "take wing to go and get water, flying generally low ; and when they find any thoroughfare, through a wood or range of trees, they

Went through the army, cheering up the soldiers.

K. Rich. So, I am satisfied. — Give me a bowl of wine :
I have not that alacrity of spirit,
Nor cheer of mind, that I was wont to have. [*Wine brought.*
Well, set it down. — Is ink and paper ready?

Rat. It is, my lord.

K. Rich. Bid my guard watch; leave me. — Ratcliff,
About the mid of night come to my tent
And help to arm me. — Leave me, I say.

> [*King* RICHARD, *retires into his tent, and sleeps.*
> *Exeunt* RATCLIFF *and others.*

RICHMOND'S *tent opens, and discovers him and his* Officers, *&c.*
Enter STANLEY.

Stan. Fortune and victory sit on thy helm !

Richm. All comfort that the dark night can afford
Be to thy person, noble father-in-law !
Tell me, how fares our loving mother?

Stan. I, by attorney, bless thee from thy mother,
Who prays continually for Richmond's good :
So much for that. — The silent hours steal on,
And flaky darkness breaks within the East.
In brief, — for so the season bids us be, —
Prepare thy battle early in the morning,
And put thy fortune to th' arbitrement
Of bloody strokes and mortal-staring war.[10]

---

venture through." The artificial glades made for them to pass through
were called *cock*-roads. Hence *cock-shut time* and *cock-shut light* were
used to express the evening twilight.

[10] "*Mortal staring* war" sounds rather odd and harsh, but probably
means war looking with *deadly* eye, or staring *fatally*, on its victims. So
the Poet very often uses *mortal* for that which *kills*, not that which *dies*.

I, as I may,—that which I would I cannot,—
With best advantage will deceive the time,
And aid thee in this doubtful shock of arms:
But on thy side I may not be too forward,
Lest, being seen, thy brother, tender George,
Be executed in his father's sight.
Farewell: the leisure [11] and the fearful time
Cuts off the ceremonious vows of love
And ample interchange of sweet discourse,
Which so-long-sunder'd friends should dwell upon:
God give us leisure for these rites of love!
Once more, adieu: be valiant, and speed well!

 Richm. Good lords, conduct him to his regiment:
I'll strive, with troubled thoughts, to take a nap,
Lest leaden slumber peise [12] me down to-morrow,
When I should mount with wings of victory:
Once more, good night, kind lords and gentlemen.—

      [*Exeunt* Officers, *&c., with* STANLEY.

O Thou, whose captain I account myself,
Look on my forces with a gracious eye;
Put in their hands Thy bruising irons of wrath,
That they may crush down with a heavy fall
Th' usurping helmets of our adversaries!
Make us Thy ministers of chastisement,
That we may praise Thee in the victory!
To Thee I do commend my watchful soul,
Ere I let fall the windows of mine eyes:

---

11 We still have a phrase equivalent to this, however harsh it may seem:
"I would do this if *leisure* would permit"; where *leisure* stands for *want
of leisure.* So in *King Richard II.,* i. 1: "Which then our *leisure would
not let* us hear." See *As You Like It,* page 79, note 7.

 12 *Peise* is an old form of *poise, weigh;* much used in the Poet's time.

Sleeping and waking, O, defend me still !   [*Sleeps.*

The Ghost of Prince EDWARD, *son to King* HENRY *the Sixth,*
rises between the two tents.

    Ghost of P. E. [*To K.* RICH.] Let me sit heavy on thy
        soul to-morrow !
Think, how thou stabb'dst me in my prime of youth
At Tewksbury : despair, therefóre, and die !—
[*To* RICHM.] Be cheerful, Richmond ; for the wrongèd souls
Of butcher'd princes fight in thy behalf :
King Henry's issue, Richmond, comforts thee.

      The Ghost of King HENRY *the Sixth rises.*

    Ghost of K. H. [*To K.* RICH.] When I was mortal, my
        anointed body
By thee was punchèd full of deadly holes :
Think on the Tower and me : despair, and die ;
Harry the Sixth bids thee despair and die !—
[*To* RICHM.] Virtuous and holy, be thou conqueror !
Harry, that prophesied thou shouldst be king,
Doth comfort thee in sleep : live thou, and flourish !

        The Ghost of CLARENCE *rises.*

    Ghost of C. [*To K.* RICH.] Let me sit heavy on thy soul
        to-morrow !
I, that was wash'd to death with fulsome wine,[13]
Poor Clarence, by thy guile betray'd to death !

---

   [13] *Fulsome* probably has reference to the qualities of Malmsey wine,
which was peculiarly sweet and luscious, so much so as to cloy the appetite
after a little drinking. — The Poet has represented Clarence as having been
killed before he was thrown into the butt of wine. But one report gave it
that he was drowned in such a cask of drink.

To-morrow in the battle think on me,
And fall thy edgeless sword : despair, and die !—
[*To* RICHM.] Thou offspring of the House of Lancaster,
The wrongèd heirs of York do pray for thee :
Good angels guard thy battle ! live, and flourish !

    The Ghosts of RIVERS, GREY, *and* VAUGHAN, *rise.*

    Ghost of R.   [*To K.* RICH.]   Let me sit heavy on thy soul
        to-morrow,
Rivers, that died at Pomfret ! despair, and die !
    Ghost of G.   [*To K.* RICH.]   Think upon Grey, and let
        thy soul despair !
    Ghost of V.   [*To K.* RICH.]   Think upon Vaughan, and,
        with guilty fear,
Let fall thy pointless lance : despair, and die !
    All three.   [*To* RICHM.]   Awake, and think our wrongs in
        Richard's bosom
Will conquer him ! awake, and win the day !

    The Ghost of HASTINGS *rises.*

    Ghost of H.   [*To K.* RICH.]   Bloody and guilty, guiltily
        awake,
And in a bloody battle end thy days !
Think on Lord Hastings : so despair, and die !—
[*To* RICHM.]   Quiet untroubled soul, awake, awake !
Arm, fight, and conquer, for fair England's sake !

    The Ghosts of the two young Princes *rise.*

    Ghosts of the two P.   [*To K.* RICH.]   Dream on thy
        cousins smother'd in the Tower :
Let us be lead within thy bosom, Richard,
And weigh thee down to ruin, shame, and death !

Thy nephews' souls bid thee despair and die !—

[*To* RICHM.] Sleep, Richmond, sleep in peace, and wake
        in joy;

Good angels guard thee from the boar's annoy !

Live, and beget a happy race of kings !

Edward's unhappy sons do bid thee flourish.

The Ghost of Queen ANNE rises.

Ghost of Q. A. [*To* K. RICH.] Richard, thy wife, that
        wretched Anne thy wife,

That never slept a quiet hour with thee,

Now fills thy sleep with perturbations :

To-morrow in the battle think on me,

And fall thy edgeless sword : despair, and die !—

[*To* RICHM.] Thou quiet soul, sleep thou a quiet sleep;

Dream of success and happy victory !

Thy adversary's wife doth pray for thee.

The Ghost of BUCKINGHAM rises.

Ghost of B. [*To* K. RICH.] The first was I that help'd
        thee to the crown ;

The last was I that felt thy tyranny :

O, in the battle think on Buckingham,

And die in terror of thy guiltiness !

Dream on, dream on, of bloody deeds and death :

Fainting, despair ; despairing, yield thy breath !—

[*To* RICHM.] I died for hope [14] ere I could lend thee aid :

But cheer thy heart, and be thou not dismay'd :

God and good angels fight on Richmond's side !

---

[14] Buckingham's *hope* of aiding Richmond induced him to take up arms :
he lost his life in consequence, and therefore may be said to have died *for*
hope; hope being the *cause* which led to that event.

And Richard fall in height of all his pride![15]

      [*The Ghosts vanish.   King* RICHARD *starts out*
                                        of his dream.

   K. Rich. Give me another horse,—bind up my wounds,—
Have mercy, Jesu!—Soft! I did but dream.—
O coward conscience, how dost thou afflict me!—
The lights burn blue.—It is now dead midnight.
Cold fearful drops stand on my trembling flesh.
What do I fear? myself? there's none else by:
Richard loves Richard; that is, I am I.
Is there a murderer here? No;—yes, I am:
Then fly. What, from myself? Great reason why,—
Lest I revenge myself upon myself.
Alack, I love myself. Wherefore? for any good
That I myself have done unto myself?
O, no! alas, I rather hate myself
For hateful deeds committed by myself!
I am a villain: yet I lie, I am not.
Fool, of thyself speak well:—fool, do not flatter.
My conscience hath a thousand several tongues,
And every tongue brings in a several tale,
And every tale condemns me for a villain.
Perjury, perjury, in the high'st degree;

[15] In this series of speeches the Poet has with happy effect given a "local habitation and a name" to what is thus stated in the *Chronicles :* "The fame went, that he had the same night a terrible dreame; for it seemed to him, being asleepe, that he did see diverse images like terrible divels, which pulled and haled him, not suffering him to take anie quiet or rest. The which strange vision not so suddenlie strake his heart with feare, but it stuffed his head with many busie and dreadfull imaginations. For incontinent after, his heart being almost damped, he prognosticated the doubtfull chance of the battle, not using the alacritie and mirth of mind and countenance as he was accustomed to doo."

Murder, stern murder, in the direst degree ;
All several sins, all used in each degree,
Throng to the bar, crying all *Guilty! guilty!*
I shall despair.   There is no creature loves me ;
And, if I die, no soul shall pity me :
Nay, wherefore should they, since that I myself
Find in myself no pity to myself?[16]

Re-enter RATCLIFF.

Rat. My lord,—
K. Rich. Who's there?
Rat. My lord, 'tis I.   The early village-cock
Hath twice done salutation to the morn ;
Your friends are up, and buckle on their armour.
K. Rich. O Ratcliff, I have dream'd a fearful dream !
What thinkest thou, will our friends prove all true?
Rat. No doubt, my lord.
K. Rich.   O Ratcliff, I fear, I fear !
Methought the souls of all that I had murder'd
Came to my tent ; and every one did threat
To-morrow's vengeance on the head of Richard.
Rat. Nay, good my lord, be not afraid of shadows.
K. Rich. By the apostle Paul, shadows to-night
Have struck more terror to the soul of Richard
Than can the substance of ten thousand soldiers
Armèd in proof [17] and led by shallow Richmond.
It is not yet near day.   Come, go with me ;

[16] In this strange speech there are some ten lines in or near the Poet's
best style; the others are in his worst; so inferior indeed, that it is not easy
to understand how Shakespeare could have written them at all.

[17] "Armèd in *proof*" is encased in armour that is proof against warlike
weapons.   Probably the phrase is meant to include offensive as well as de-
fensive armour.

Under our tents I'll play the eaves-dropper,
To hear if any mean to shrink from me.

> [*Exeunt King* RICHARD *and* RATCLIFF.

Re-enter OXFORD, *with other* Lords, *&c.*

Lords. Good morrow, Richmond!

Richm. [*Waking.*] Cry mercy, lords and watchful gentlemen,
That you have ta'en a tardy sluggard here.

Lords. How have you slept, my lord?

Richm. The sweetest sleep, and fairest-boding dreams
That ever enter'd in a drowsy head,
Have I since your departure had, my lords.
Methought their souls, whose bodies Richard murder'd,
Came to my tent, and cried, *On! victory!*
I promise you, my heart is very jocund
In the remembrance of so fair a dream.
How far into the morning is it, lords?

Lords. Upon the stroke of four.

Richm. Why, then 'tis time to arm and give direction. —

> [*He advances to the Troops.*

More than I have said, loving countrymen,
The leisure [18] and enforcement of the time
Forbids to dwell upon: yet remember this,
God and our good cause fight upon our side;
The prayers of holy saints and wrongèd souls,
Like high-rear'd bulwarks, stand before our faces;
Richard except, those whom we fight against
Had rather have us win than him they follow:
For what is he they follow? truly, gentlemen,
A bloody tyrant and a homicide;

---

[18] *Leisure*, again, for *want of leisure*. See page 187, note 11.

One raised in blood, and one in blood establish'd ;
One that made means to come by what he hath,
And slaughter'd those that were the means to help him ;
A base foul stone, made precious by the foil
Of England's chair, where he is falsely set ;[19]
One that hath ever been God's enemy :
Then, if you fight against God's enemy,
God will, in justice, ward you as His soldiers ;
If you do sweat to put a tyrant down,
You sleep in peace, the tyrant being slain ;
If you do fight against your country's foes,
Your country's fat shall pay your pains the hire ;
If you do fight in safeguard of your wives,
Your wives shall welcome home the conquerors ;
If you do free your children from the sword,
Your children's children quit[20] it in your age.
Then, in the name of God and all these rights,
Advance your standards, draw your willing swords.
For me, the ransom of my bold attempt
Shall be this cold corpse on the earth's cold face ;
But if I thrive, the gain of my attempt
The least of you shall share his part thereof.—
Sound drums and trumpets, boldly, cheerfully ;
God and Saint George ! Richmond and victory !   [*Exeunt.*

Re-enter King RICHARD, RATCLIFF, *Attendants, and Forces.*

   K. Rich. What said Northumberland as touching Rich-
      mond?

   Rat. That he was never trainèd up in arms.

---

19 " England's *chair* " is the *throne*. The allusion is to the practice of
setting gems of little worth, with a bright-coloured *foil* under them.

20 *Quit*, again, in the sense of *requite*. See page 157, note 3.

K. Rich. He said the truth : and what said Surrey then?

Rat. He smiled, and said, *The better for our purpose.*

K. Rich. He was i' the right ; and so indeed it is. —

[Clock strikes.

Tell the clock there. — Give me a calendar. —

Who saw the Sun to-day?

Rat.   Not I, my lord.

K. Rich. Then he disdains to shine ; for, by the book,

He should have braved [21] the East an hour ago :

A black day will it be to somebody. —

Ratcliff, —

Rat. My lord?

K. Rich.   The Sun will not be seen to-day ;

The sky doth frown and lour upon our army.

I would these dewy tears were from the ground.

Not shine to-day !   Why, what is that to me

More than to Richmond? for the selfsame heaven

That frowns on me looks sadly upon him.

Enter NORFOLK.

Nor. Arm, arm, my lord ; the foe vaunts in the field.

K. Rich. Come, bustle, bustle ; — caparison my horse ; —

Call up Lord Stanley, bid him bring his power :

I will lead forth my soldiers to the plain,

And thus my battle shall be orderéd :

My foreward shall be drawn out all in length,

Consisting equally of Horse and Foot ;

Our archers shall be placéd in the midst :

John Duke of Norfolk, Thomas Earl of Surrey,

Shall have the leading of this Foot and Horse.

They thus directed, we ourself will follow

---

[21] To *brave* is, in one of its senses, to *make fine, splendid,* or *glorious.*

In the main battle ; whose puissance on either side
Shall be well wingèd with our chiefest Horse.
This, and Saint George to boot ![22]—What think'st thou,
    Norfolk?

  Nor. A good direction, warlike sovereign.—
This found I on my tent this morning.   [*Giving a scroll.*

  K. Rich. [Reads.] *Jockey of Norfolk, be not too bold,*
For Dickon thy master is bought and sold.[23]

A thing devisèd by the enemy.—
Go, gentlemen, every man unto his charge :
Let not our babbling dreams affright our souls ;
Conscience is but a word that cowards use,
Devised at first to keep the strong in awe :
Our strong arms be our conscience, swords our law.
March on, join bravely, let us to't pell-mell ;
If not to Heaven, then hand in hand to Hell.—
[*To his* Soldiers.] What shall I say more than I have inferr'd ?[24]
Remember whom you are to cope withal ;
A sort[25] of vagabonds, rascals, and runaways,

---

[22] This, and Saint George to help us, into the bargain.

[23] So in the *Chronicles :* " John duke of Norffolke was warned by diverse
to refrain from the field, insomuch that the night before he should set forward toward the king, one wrote this rime upon his gate :

> Jocke of Norffolke, be not too bold,
> For Dickon thy maister is bought and sold."

Jocky and *Dickon* were familiar forms of *John* and *Richard.* — *Bought and
sold* was a sort of proverbial phrase for *hopelessly ruined by treacherous
practices.*

[24] Here again we have *inferr'd* for *brought forward* or *alleged.*

[25] *Sort* here means *crew, pack,* or *set.* So in *2 Henry VI.,* iii. 2: "He
was the lord ambassador sent from a *sort* of tinkers to the King." And in
A Midsummer-Night's Dream, iii. 2, Puck describes Bottom as " the shal-
lowest thickskin of that barren *sort*"; referring to the " crew of patches "
who are getting up the interlude of *Pyramus and Thisbe.*

A scum of Bretagnes, and base lacquey peasants,
Whom their o'er-cloyèd country vomits forth
To desperate ventures and assured destruction.
You sleeping safe, they bring to you unrest ;
You having lands, and bless'd with beauteous wives,
They would distrain[26] the one, distain the other.
And who doth lead them but a paltry fellow,
Long kept in Bretagne at our mother's cost?[27]
A milk-sop, one that never in his life
Felt so much cold as over shoes in snow?
Let's whip these stragglers o'er the seas again ;
Lash hence these overweening rags of France,
These famish'd beggars, weary of their lives ;
Who, but for dreaming on this fond exploit,
For want of means, poor rats, had hang'd themselves :
If we be conquer'd, let men conquer us,
And not these bastard Bretagnes ; whom our fathers
Have in their own land beaten, bobb'd, and thump'd,
And, on recórd, left them the heirs of shame.
Shall these enjoy our lands? [*Drum afar off.*] Hark ! I hear
      their drum. —
Fight, gentlemen of England ! fight, bold yeomen !

   [26] *Distrain* is here used in its old sense of *lawless seizure*. See *King Richard II.*, page 94, note 13.

   [27] This should be "at our *brother's* cost." Richmond was in fact held in a sort of honourable custody at the Duke of Bretagne's Court, his means being supplied by Charles, Duke of Burgundy, who was Richard's brother-in-law. Hall gives the matter thus : "And to begyn with the earle of Richmond Captaine of this rebellion, he is a Welsh mylkesoppe, a man of small courage, and of lesse experience in marcyall acts and feates of warr, brought up by my brothers meanes and myne like a captive in a close cage in the court of Frances duke of Britaine." Holinshed copied Hall's account, but in Holinshed's second edition "*moothers* meanes" got misprinted for "*brothers* meanes"; and hence the Poet's mistake.

Draw, archers, draw your arrows to the head !
Spur your proud horses hard, and ride in blood ;
Amaze the welkin with your broken staves ![28] —

Enter a Messenger.

What says Lord Stanley? will he bring his power?
    Mess. My lord, he doth deny to come.
    K. Rich. Off with his son George's head !
    Nor. My lord, the enemy is past the marsh : [29]
After the battle let George Stanley die.
    K. Rich. A thousand hearts are great within my bosom :
Advance our standards, set upon our foes ;
Our ancient word of courage, fair Saint George,
Inspire us with the spleen of fiery dragons !
Upon them !   Victory sits on our helms.   [*Exeunt.*

SCENE IV. — *Another Part of the Field.*

Alarums : excursions.   Enter NORFOLK *and Forces ; to him*
CATESBY.

    Cate. Rescue, my Lord of Norfolk, rescue, rescue !
The King enacts more wonders than a man,
Daring an opposite to every danger : [1]

[28] Fright the skies with the shivers of your lances.
[29] Betweene both armies there was a great marish, which the earle of Richmond left on his right hand; for this intent, that it should be on that side a defense for his part, and in so dooing he had the sunne at his backe, and in the faces of his enimies.   When king Richard saw the earles companie was passed the marish, he did command with all hast to set upon them. — HOLINSHED.
[1] The Poet repeatedly uses *opposite* for *opponent* or *adversary.* So that "daring an opposite to every danger" probably means *offering himself as an opponent in* every danger, or, which comes to the same thing, challenging every dangerous antagonist to fight with him.

His horse is slain, and all on foot he fights,
Seeking for Richmond in the throat of death.
Rescue, fair lord, or else the day is lost!

Alarums. Enter King RICHARD.

K. Rich. A horse! a horse! my kingdom for a horse!
Cate. Withdraw, my lord; I'll help you to a horse.
K. Rich. Slave, I have set my life upon a cast,
And I will stand the hazard of the die:
I think there be six Richmonds in the field;
Five have I slain to-day instead of him.² —
A horse! a horse! my kingdom for a horse!   [*Exeunt.*

SCENE V. — *Another Part of the Field.*

Alarums. Enter, from opposite sides, King RICHARD *and*
RICHMOND; *they fight, and exeunt fighting. Retreat and
flourish. Then re-enter* RICHMOND, *with* STANLEY *bearing
the crown, and divers other* Lords, *and Forces.*

Richm. God and your arms be praised, victorious friends;
The day is ours, the bloody dog is dead.

² Shakespeare employs this incident with historical propriety in The
First Part of *King Henry IV*. He had here also good ground for his
poetical exaggeration. Richard, according to the *Chronicles*, was determined if possible to engage with Richmond in single combat. For this
purpose he rode furiously to that quarter of the field where the Earl was;
attacked his standard bearer, Sir William Brandon, and killed him; then
assaulted Sir John Cheney, whom he overthrew. Having thus at length
cleared his way to his antagonist, he engaged in single combat with him,
and probably would have been victorious, but that at that instant Sir
William Stanley with three thousand men joined Richmond's army, and
the royal forces fled with great precipitation. Richard was soon afterwards
overpowered by numbers, and fell, fighting bravely to the last.

Stan. Courageous Richmond, well hast thou acquit[3] thee.
Lo, here, this long-usurpèd royalty
From the dead temples of this bloody wretch
Have I pluck'd off, to grace thy brows withal:
Wear it, enjoy it, and make much of it.

Richm. Great God of Heaven, say Amen to all!—
But, tell me now, is young George Stanley living?

Stan. He is, my lord, and safe in Leicester town;
Whither, if 't please you, we may now withdraw us.

Richm. What men of name are slain on either side?

Stan. John Duke of Norfolk, Walter Lord Ferrers,
Sir Robert Brakenbury, and Sir William Brandon.

Richm. Inter their bodies as becomes their births:
Proclaim a pardon to the soldiers fled
That in submission will return to us:
And then, as we have ta'en the Sacrament,
We will unite the white rose and the red:—
Smile Heaven upon this fair conjunction,
That long hath frown'd upon their enmity!—
What traitor hears me, and says not Amen?
England hath long been mad and scarr'd herself;
The brother blindly shed the brother's blood,
The father rashly slaughter'd his own son,
The son, compell'd, been butcher to the sire:
All this divided York and Lancaster,
O, now let Richmond and Elizabeth,
The true succeeders of each royal House,—
Divided in their dire division,—
By God's fair ordinance conjoin together!
And let their heirs—God, if Thy will be so—

---

[3] *Acquit* for *acquitted.*   See page 85, note 14, and page 122, note 2.

Enrich the time to come with smooth-faced peace,
With smiling plenty, and fair prosperous days !
Abate [4] the edge of traitors, gracious Lord,
That would reduce [5] these bloody days again,
And make poor England weep in streams of blood !
Let them not live to taste this land's increase
That would with treason wound this fair land's peace !
Now civil wounds are stopp'd, peace lives again :
That she may long live here, God say Amen !   [*Exeunt.*

---

[4] *Abate* here means *make dull*, like *rebate*. So, in *Love's Labours Lost*,
i. 1 : " That honour which shall '*bate* his scythe's keen edge." Also, in the
novel of *Pericles*, 1608 : " Absence *abates* that edge that presence whets."
And Florio : " Spontare, — *to abate the edge or point of any thing or weapon, to blunt, to unpoint.*"

[5] *Reduce*, again, in the Latin sense of *bring back*. See page 98, note 10.

CRITICAL NOTES.

—◆—

Page 49. *That* tempers *him to this extremity*. — So the quarto of 1597. The quarto of 1598 corrupted *tempers* into *tempts*, thus leaving the verse defective; and the folio, to complete the verse, printed "That *tempts* him to this *harsh* Extremity."

P. 49. *Beseech your Graces both to pardon me.* — The old copies have "*I* beseech." In such phrases as "I beseech," "I pray," &c., the elision of the pronoun is too common in Shakespeare to need any special remark.

P. 50. *Well struck in years, fair, and not* jealous. — The folio has *jealious;* and, as a trisyllable is wanted here to complete the verse, perhaps it should be printed so. Walker asks, "Why not write *jealious* in this place?"

P. 50. *And the Queen's kindred are made gentlefolks.* — The old copies read "And *that* the Queenes Kindred." But the repetition of *that* is needless as regards the sense, and defeats the rhythm of the line.

P. 50. *Beseech your Grace to pardon me.* — Here, again, the old editions have "*I* beseech," and "*I do* beseech."

P. 52. *Till George be pack'd with post-*haste *up to Heaven.* — So Collier's second folio. The old copies have *post-horse* instead of *post-haste.* In support of the old reading, Dyce quotes from the Induction to *2 King Henry IV.*, where Rumour speaks of "Making the wind my *post-horse.*" But it seems to me that the two cases are by no means parallel: there the *instrument* of motion was to be expressed, here the *manner.*

ACT I., SCENE 2.

P. 58. *Thou wast the cause, and most accursed* th' effect. — So
Hanmer.   The old text reads "Thou was't the cause, and most accurst
effect."

P. 58.   *To undertake the death of all the world,*
          So I might live *one hour in your sweet bosom.* — So the folio.
The quartos have *rest* instead of *live*.   Lettsom would change *live* to
lie, as the two words were often confounded.   But *live* was probably
meant in antithesis to *death* in the line before.

P. 59.   Not *when my father York and Edward wept.* — So Pope.
The folio has *No* instead of *Not*.   The line is not in the quartos.

P. 62.   *With curses in her mouth, tears in her eyes,*
          The bleeding witness of her *hatred by.* — So the quartos.   The
folio has "witness of *my* hatred," which some editors prefer.   But
"witness of *my* hatred" to what?   Richard is speaking of the causes
which the Lady Anne has for hating himself, and he regards King
Henry's death as one of them, and the presence of Henry's bleeding
corse is a witness to that hatred.

P. 63.   *Young,* wise, and valiant, *and, no doubt, right royal.* — So
Pope.   The old text reads "Yong, *Valiant, Wise,* and (no doubt)
right Royal."   Surely there ought to be no hitch or halting in the metre
here.   Various ways of rectifying the verse have been proposed, but
Pope's is the simplest.

ACT I., SCENE 3.

P. 64.   *Here come the Lords of Buckingham and* Stanley. — Here
and four times afterwards in this scene, as also in several other places,
the old editions have *Derby* instead of *Stanley;* but they have *Stanley*
in a still larger number of places.   In fact, the Lord Stanley of this
play did not become Earl of Derby till after the accession of Henry
VII.   For this confusion of names or titles in the old copies it is not

easy to account; but it seems hardly credible that it could have origi-
nated with Shakespeare: at all events, I can see no sufficient reason
for retaining it in the text, as some editors do.

P. 67.   *That thereby he may gather*
          The ground of your ill-will, and so remove it. — The quartos
have " and *to* remove it." The correction is Capell's. The folio has
merely "that he may learne the ground," omitting the rest.

P. 70. As *little joy enjoys the Queen thereof.* — The old copies have
"*A* little joy." But *A* is no doubt a misprint for *As;* for Margaret is
running a variation upon what Elizabeth has just said, and the latter
began her speech with "*As* little joy."

P. 73. *Thou that wast seal'd in thy nativity*
          The *slave* *of Nature and the* son *of Hell.* — It appears that
some have stumbled at the words *slave* and *son* here. Collier's second
folio has " The *stain* of nature and the *scorn* of Hell "; Singer's, " The
shame of nature and the *spawn* of Hell." For my part, I have to confess that the words have never troubled me; and I think Walker is
right in saying that a *slave of nature* means " neither more nor less
than a *born villain.*"

P. 75. Riv. *Peace, peace, for shame, if not for charity.* — The old
text assigns this speech to Buckingham. But Margaret's reply to it,
and her next speech, which is addressed to Buckingham, show that the
prefix "*Buc.*" must be wrong. Walker points out the error, and Lettsom remarks that perhaps the speech should be given to Rivers.

ACT I., SCENE 4.

P. 81. Brak. *I will, my lord: God give your Grace good rest !* —
          Sorrow breaks seasons and reposing hours, &c. — So the
quartos. Between these two lines, the folio has "*Enter Brakenbury
the Lieutenant,*" and prefixes "*Bra.*" to the second line ; the preceding
dialogue being between Clarence and the "*Keeper,*" and having "*Enter
Clarence and Keeper*" at the opening of the scene. Of course this is

making the Lieutenant and the Keeper two distinct persons. Why the folio made this change upon the quartos, is not very apparent, there being nothing gained by such variety of speakers. I must add that, in the last speech of Clarence before the entrance of Brakenbury, the folio has "*Ah Keeper, Keeper,* I have done *these* things," instead of "*O Brakenbury,* I have done *those* things." Also, in Brakenbury's speech a little after, the folio has "*There lies* the Duke asleepe, *and there* the keys," instead of "*Here are* the keys; *there sits* the duke asleep." White objects to the quarto arrangement and reading, that " it was a violation of all propriety to make Sir Robert Brakenbury, Lieutenant of the Tower, go about with a bunch of ponderous keys at his girdle or in his hand." But why may not the Lieutenant have taken the keys from one of his subordinates, for the purpose of visiting Clarence? And is there not quite as much impropriety in making Clarence, a prince of the royal blood, unbosom himself so freely in a dialogue with a mere turnkey of the prison?

P. 83. *I hope* my holy *humour will change.* — So the quartos. The folio "*this passionate* humor *of mine.*" Here, again, I prefer the quarto text, because the same speaker, in his next speech, says, "some certain dregs of *conscience* are yet within me."

P. 88. Hast thou *that holy feeling in thy* soul, &c. — In the quartos, this and the three following lines are addressed to the second murderer only, and in reply to what is said by him alone just before, " Make peace with God." The folio reads "*Have you* that holy feeling in your *soules,*" &c., and makes the whole speech an address to both the Murderers.

P. 88. 2 Murd. *What shall we do?*
　　　Clar.　　　　　　　　　　*Relent, and save your souls.*
　　　1 Murd. *Relent! 'tis cowardly and womanish.*
　　　Clar. *Not to relent is beastly, savage, devilish.* —
My friend, I spy some pity in thy looks;
O, if thine eye be not a flatterer,
Come thou on my side, and entreat for me:
A begging prince what beggar pities not?

I Murd. *Ay*, [Stabbing him.] *thus, and thus*, &c. — So the first quarto, which is followed by Capell, Staunton, and Dyce in his last edition. The other quartos have the same, with only some slight variations. The folio has the following:

> 2. Whall shall we do?
> Cla. Relent, and save your soules:
> *Which of you, if you were a Princes Sonne,*
> *Being pent from Liberty, as I am now,*
> *If two such murtherers as your selves came to you,*
> *Would not intreat for life, as you would begge*
> *Were you in my distresse.*
> 1. Relent? *no :* 'Tis cowardly and womanish.
> Cla. Not to relent, is beastly, savage, divellish:
> My Friend, I spy some pitty in thy lookes:
> O, if thine eye be not a Flatterer,
> Come thou on my side, and intreate for mee,
> A begging Prince, what begger pitties not.
> 2. *Looke behinde you, my Lord.*
> 1. Take *that*, and *that*, &c.

Here it is manifest that the folio additions serve no purpose but to embarrass and enfeeble the dialogue : besides, in some places it is hardly possible to make any sense out of them. To amend the latter fault, they have been variously tinkered at, but with only partial success. I therefore have no scruple of concurring with the other editors named in omitting them altogether as an unauthorized intrusion.

P. 88. *How fain, like Pilate, would I wash my hands*
    Of this most grievous murder ! — So the folio. The quartos have " Of this most grievous *guilty* murder *done*."

ACT II., SCENE I.

P. 92. *Of you, Lord Rivers, — and, Lord Grey, of you,*
    That all without desert have frown'd on me ; —
    Dukes, earls, lords, gentlemen ; — indeed, of all. — So the quartos. Between the second and third of these lines, the folio has the following line : " Of you Lord Woodvill, and Lord Scales of you." Malone pointed out the fact, that there was no such person as Lord Woodville, and that Lord Scales was the oldest son of Earl Rivers.

ACT II., SCENE 2.

P. 100. Hast. *And so in me; and so, I think, in all:* &c. — The old copies assign this speech to Rivers; which can hardly be right, as Rivers has all along been opposed to the faction who are here trying to dissemble their thoughts. The old copies also give the next speech to Hastings, which is here assigned to Stanley. The corrections are Capell's.

ACT II., SCENE 4.

P. 105. Q. Eliz.   *For what offence?*
       Mess. *The sum of all I can I have disclosed:*
Why or for what these nobles were committed
Is all unknown to me, my gracious lady. — The old copies assign the first of these speeches to the Archbishop; the quartos, with the prefix " *Car*.," the folio, with " *Arch*." But the quartos have *Lady* at the end of the next speech, while the folio has *Lord*, thus making the correction in the wrong place. Johnson detected the error.

ACT III., SCENE 1.

P. 109. *You are too senseless-obstinate, my lord,*
     Too ceremonious and traditional;
     Weigh it but with the grossness of this age.
     You break not sanctuary in seizing him: &c. — I here adopt the punctuation proposed by Heath. The pointing commonly followed, both in the old and in modern editions, sets a colon at the end of the second line, and a comma at the end of the third; thus connecting the third line with what follows, not with what precedes. With this pointing, I see no way but to accept Warburton's alteration of the text, " the *greenness* of *his* age," or something equivalent. With that change, the sense is, " If you consider the matter with due reference to the childish and tender age of the Prince, you break not sanctuary in taking him away." Here we have no want of logical coherence; but, with the old reading and the old pointing, no such coherence seems possible. The passage has troubled editors a good deal; and other textual changes have been proposed: Collier's second folio has

" the *goodness* of *his* age "; and Lettsom notes that " the context seems to require a word like *cunning* or *knowledge*." I at one time thought that "*grossness* of this age " might refer to the *gross abuses* of sanctuary practised in that age ; but this consideration really does nothing towards healing the logical incoherence. However, as those abuses are largely insisted on in Buckingham's speech as reported by More, I subjoin a considerable extract from the latter :

Now look how few sanctuary men there be whom necessity or misfortune compelled to go thither. And then see, on the other side, what a sort there be commonly therein of such whom wilful unthriftiness hath brought to naught. What a rabble of thieves, murderers, and malicious heinous traitors there be, and that in two places specially; the one at the elbow of the city, and the other in the very bowels. I dare well avow it, *if you weigh the good that they do, with the hurt that cometh of them, ye shall find it much better to lose both than to have both.* And this I say, although they were not abused (as they now be, and long have been,) that I fear me ever they will be, while men be afeared to set-to their hands to the amendment, as though God and Saint Peter were the patrons of ungracious living. Now unthrifts riot and run in debt upon boldness of these places; yea, rich men run thither with poor men's goods; there they build, there they spend, and bid their creditors go whistle. Men's wives run thither with their husbands' plate, and say they dare not abide with their husbands for beating: thieves bring thither stolen goods, and live thereon. There devise they new robberies nightly, and steal out and rob, reave, and kill men, and come again into those places, as though those places gave them not only a safeguard for the harm that they have done, but a license also to do more mischief. Where a man is by lawful means in peril, there needeth he the tuition of some special privilege, which is the only ground of all sanctuaries ; from which necessity this noble prince is far, whose love to his king, nature and kindred proveth ; whose innocency to all the world, his tender youth affirmeth ; and so sanctuary, as for him, is not necessary. Men come not to sanctuary as they come to baptism, to require it by his godfathers : he must ask it himself that must have it ; and reason, sith no man hath cause to have it, but whose conscience of his own fault maketh him have need to require it. What will, then, hath yonder babe, which, if he had discretion to require it, if need were, I dare say would be now right angry with them that keep him there. *And verily I have heard of sanctuary men, but I never heard before of sanctuary children. And he that taketh one out of sanctuary to do him good, I say plainly, he breaketh no sanctuary.*

P. 109. *This Prince hath neither claim'd it nor deserved it ; Therefore, in mine opinion, cannot have it.* — So the second folio. The earlier editions have "*And* therefore." Probably a repetition by mistake from the second line above, "*And* those who," &c.

P. 112. *I'd weigh it lightly, were it heavier.* — So Hanmer. The old text has "*I* weigh it lightly."

P. 112. I would, that I might thank you, as — as — you call me. —
The folio has "thank you, as, as, you call me." Modern editions
print "thank you, as you call me." Walker quotes the line as given
in the folio, and then adds, " Meaning, I suppose, ' as — as — you call
me.' May not this be the right reading ? "

P. 115. My lord, what shall we do, if we perceive
        Lord Hastings will not yield to our complots ? — The old copies
have "*Now*, my Lord, What shall wee doe." Here *Now* does nothing
but clog both sense and metre. Omitted by Pope.

Act iii., Scene 2.

P. 120. Come the next Sabbath, and I will content you. — After this
line, the folio makes the Priest answer, " Ile wait upon your Lordship."
As these are precisely the words in which Hastings is there made to
answer Buckingham a little after, it seems altogether probable that
they were inserted *twice* by mistake. The quartos lack them in both
places.

Act iii., Scene 3.

P. 122. Make haste ; the hour of death is expirate. — The first folio
has " the houre of death is *expiate*." For " is *expiate*," the second
folio substitutes " is *now expir'd*." The quartos give the whole line
thus : " Come, come, dispatch, the limit of your lives is out "; repeat-
ing a line that occurs a little before. Steevens proposed *expirate*, and
so Singer prints. The sense of *expired* is evidently wanted here ; and
I more than doubt whether *expiate* was ever used in that sense. Nor
can that sense be fairly drawn from any of the recognized meanings of
the verb *expio*, while it is one of the commonest meanings of the Latin
exspiratus or *expiratus*. It is true, the Poet's 22d *Sonnet* has " Then
look I death my days should *expiate* "; but here again I have little
doubt that *expiate* is a misprint for *expirate*.

Act iii., Scene 4.

P. 122. Buck. *Are all things ready for that royal time ?*
        Stan. They are ; *and wants but nomination. —* So Capell.
Instead of *They are*, the old text has *It is*. This was probably a soph-

istication introduced in order to make a subject for *wants*, whereas *nomination* is the subject of *wants* : " and *there* wants," or " there *is wanting* but the naming of the time."

P. 125. *What of his heart perceive you in his face*
  By any likelihood *he show'd to day*. — So the quartos. The folio has *livelyhood* instead of *likelihood*. Some editors prefer the folio reading, and support it by quoting from *All's Well that Ends Well*, i. 1 : "The tyranny of her sorrows takes all *livelihood* from her cheek"; where *livelihood* is put for *liveliness*. But it seems to me that the two cases are by no means parallel. The sense of *appearance* or *sign* is plainly required in the text; and *likelihood* may very well bear that sense.

P. 125. *Lovel and* Ratcliff, *look that it be done.* — See foot-note 10. As this scene is in London, and as in the preceding, which falls on the same day, Ratcliff is represented as being at Pomfret, Theobald here substituted *Catesby* for *Ratcliff*. But, as we have Ratcliff again in the next scene, which also falls on the same day, and as the change cannot there be made without taking too much liberty with the old text, I deem it best to let the impropriety pass. Should we undertake to rectify all the discrepancies of this sort in Shakespeare, we should be — one can hardly tell where.

ACT III., SCENE 5.

P. 129. *Because, my lord, we would have had you* hear
  The traitor speak, &c. — The old text has " we would have had you *heard*." The Poet probably wrote *heare*, and we have many instances of final *d* and final *e* confounded.

P. 130. *Even where his* raging *eye or savage heart,*
  Without control, listed to make a prey. — So the folio. The quartos have " his *lustfull* eye." Pope changed *raging* to *ranging*. But " *raging* eye " is a good classical phrase, and Dryden has it in his translation of Virgil.

ACT III., SCENE 7.

P. 134. *But, like dumb* statuas *or breathing* stones,
  Stared on each other, and look'd deadly pale. — The old text has

" dumb *statues*" ; but the verse clearly requires a trisyllable, and *statua* was often used in all sorts of writing. All the quartos, except the first two, have *breathlesse* instead of *breathing*. Rowe printed " like dumb statues or *unbreathing* stones," and Lettsom proposes " like dumb *statuas, unbreathing* stones." But "*breathing* stones" seems to me better in itself, let alone the authority of the old copies.

P. 136. *He is not* lolling *on a lewd* day-*bed.* — So Pope. The old copies have *lulling* for *lolling;* and the folio has *love-bed* instead of *day-bed*. The change of *lulling* to *lolling* is fully warranted from *Troilus and Cressida*, i. 3, where the old text has "The large Achilles, on his press'd bed *lolling*." And I can hardly think that Buckingham would hint at the late King as "lolling on a lewd *love*-bed" in the day-time.

P. 136. *But* sore *I fear me shall not win him to it.* — So Collier's second folio. The old copies have *sure* instead of *sore*. Dyce approves the change by citing from *The Merchant of Venice*, v. 1: " I'll *fear* no other thing so *sore* as keeping safe Nerissa's ring."

P. 137. *And, see, a book of prayer in his hand,* —
       True ornament *to know a holy man.* — These two lines occur only in the folio, and that has *ornaments*. The misprinting of singulars and plurals for each other was very common. Of course the meaning is, " to know a holy man *by*."

P. 138. *Her face defaced with scars of infamy,*
       Her *royal stock graft with ignoble plants,*
       And almost shoulder'd *in the swallowing gulf,* &c. — The second of these lines is not in the quartos, and the folio has "*His* royal stock," — an obvious error. In the third line, Johnson proposed to read *smoulder'd* instead of *shoulder'd*, and Walker approves of that reading. See, however, foot-note 15.

P. 139.   *But my desert*
       Unmeritable shuns *your high request.* — Walker would read *shames* instead of *shuns*. As in the old copies the word is spelt *shunnes*, it might easily be a misprint for *shames*. But *shuns* yields an

apt and forcible sense ; though the proposed change seems well worth considering.

P. 141. *I am not made of* stone. — The old copies have *stones ;* another clear instance of a plural misprinted for a singular.

ACT IV., SCENE 1.

P. 143. *Now, for my life, she's wandering to the Tower,*
    On pure heart's love, to greet the tender Princes. — These lines are not in the quartos, and the folio has "the tender *Prince.*" But Anne herself says a little after, that she is going to the Tower, "To gratulate the gentle *Princes* there." The correction is Theobald's.

ACT IV., SCENE 4.

P. 157. *When didst Thou sleep* while *such a deed was done ?* — Instead of *while,* the old text repeats *when ;* probably by accident. The correction is Lettsom's.

P. 158. *I had an Edward, till a Richard kill'd him ;*
    I had a Harry, *till a Richard kill'd him.* — So the Cambridge Editors. In the second line, the quartos have *Richard* instead of *Harry,* and the folio substitutes *husband* for *Richard.* A little before, Margaret says, "When holy *Harry* died," and the Duchess, a little after, "O *Harry's* wife, triúmph not in my woes ! "

P. 158. *That foul defacer of God's handiwork ;*
    That excellent grand tyrant of the Earth,
    That reigns in gallèd eyes of weeping souls. — The last two of these lines are not in the quartos, and the folio has them transposed. An unquestionable error, which was corrected by Capell.

P. 161. *For joyful mother, one that wails the name ;*
    For queen, a very caitiff crown'd with care ;
    For one being sued-to, one that humbly sues ;
    For one commanding all, obey'd of none ;
    For one that scorn'd at me, now scorn'd of me ;

Thus hath the course of justice wheel'd about. — So the quartos, which are followed by Capell, Staunton, and Dyce. The folio has, instead of the lines in Roman type, the following:

> For one being sued too, one that humbly sues:
> For Queene, a very Caytiffe, crown'd with care:
> For she that scorn'd at me, now scorn'd of me:
> For she being feared of all, now fearing one:
> For she commanding all, obey'd of none.

P. 168. *Even* I: what *think you of it*, madam ? — Such is the reading of the quartos, except that they have "*I* even I." The folio has "Even *so : How* thinke you of it ?"

P. 168. *Send to her, by the man that slew her brothers,*
    A pair of bleeding hearts ; thereon engraved
    Edward and York. — The old copies have "thereon *ingrave.*" Collier's second folio has "thereon *engraven,*" which gives the same sense. I prefer *engraved*, because we have very frequent instances of final *d* and final *e* confounded.

P. 168. *The purple sap from her sweet brothers'* bodies. — This line is not in the quartos, and the folio has *body* instead of bodies.

P. 168. *Nay, then indeed she cannot choose but* love *thee.* — This line also is wanting in the quartos, and the folio has *hate* instead of *love*, thus giving a sense not at all suited to the context. The correction is Tyrwhitt's.

P. 169. *Advantaging their* loan *with interest.* — Not in the quartos. The folio has *Love* instead of *loan.* Corrected by Theobald.

P. 171. *Say, I, her sovereign, am her subject* now. — So Pope. The quartos have *love*, the folio *low*, instead of *now*.

P. 172. *The unity the King* thy *brother made.* — So the seventh quarto. The earlier quartos have "the King *my* brother made," — a palpable error, for which the folio substituted "the King my *husband* made."

P. 172. *As I intend to prosper and repent,*
   So thrive I in my dangerous affairs
      Of hostile arms. — So the folio. The quartos have *attempt* instead of *affairs*. I prefer the latter, because it seems more in keeping with the idea of hostile arms used defensively.

P. 173. *And be not* peevish-fond *in great designs.* — The quartos have " be not *peevish, fond* " ; the folio, " be not *peevish found.*" See foot-note 36.

ACT V., SCENE 2.

P. 181. *The* wretched, *bloody, and usurping boar,*
   That spoils your summer fields and fruitful vines,
   Swills your warm blood like wash, and makes his trough
      In your embowell'd bosoms, &c. — So Capell. The old copies have *spoil'd* instead of *spoils.* Shakespeare has indeed other like instances of abrupt change of tense, but here the change makes a bad hitch in the sense. — Some have stumbled at the word *wretched* in the first of these lines. Collier's second folio substitutes *reckless,* and Walker pronounces *wretched* " palpably wrong." But *wretched,* I think, may very well bear the sense of *hateful* or *cursed,* or nearly that ; and so the Poet elsewhere uses it ; as in *Othello,* v. 1, where Roderigo, on receiving his death-wound from Iago, exclaims, " O *wretched* villain ! "

ACT V., SCENE 3.

P. 184. K. Rich. *What is't o'clock ?*
   Cate.   *It's supper-time, my lord ;*
      It's nine *o'clock.* — So the folio. The quartos have *sixe* instead of *nine.* *Six o'clock* disorders the time of the scene; for Richmond has before said the " weary Sun hath made a golden set," and at that season, August, the Sun did not set till after seven. We are not to suppose, though, that *nine o'clock* was the usual *supper-time* at that period : on the contrary, Harrison tells us in the *Preface* to Holinshed, "The nobilitie, gentrie, and students ordinarilie go to dinner at *eleven* before noone, and to supper at *five,* or betweene five and six, at afternoone." Verplanck remarks upon the matter thus : " It seems, then, that the Poet, perceiving that the conduct of the scene required a later

hour, and wishing to preserve the incident of Richard's refusing to sup, altered the time to what, though not the common supper hour, might well be that of an army, which had just encamped, after a march."

P. 184.   *I will not sup to-night.* —
        What, is my beaver easier than it was? — So Pope, Hanmer, and Capell. Between these two lines, the old text has the hemistich, "Give me some ink and paper," — the same words that Richmond has used a little before. Here the words are at least useless, as Richard says, a little after, "Is ink and paper ready?" How the words got repeated here, is not easy to say: Capell thinks the printers put them in by mistake, "from having their eye caught by a line opposite."

P. 186. Well, *set it down.* — *Is ink and paper ready?* — The old text is without the word *Well*, thus making bad work with the metre of the line. Pope mended the breach by inserting *There;* Capell, by inserting *So.*

P. 188. *Harry, that prophesied thou shouldst be king,*
        Doth comfort thee in sleep: live thou, *and flourish!* — So Rowe and Collier's second folio. The old text omits *thou* in the second line.

P. 189. *Let fall thy* pointless *lance: despair, and die!* — So Collier's second folio. The old text lacks *pointless.* Some epithet is plainly needful here. Capell inserted *hurtless.*

P. 189. *Think on Lord Hastings:* so *despair, and die!* — So Collier's second folio. The old text lacks *so.* Pope completed the verse by inserting *and.*

P. 190. *To-morrow in the battle think on me,*
        And fall thy edgeless *sword: despair, and die!* — Here Collier's second folio has *powerless arm* for *edgeless sword.* Dyce thinks the latter is "an accidental repetition from the speech of Clarence's ghost."

P. 191. *Then fly. What, from myself? Great reason why,* —
        Lest I revenge myself upon myself. — The old copies have the

second line thus: "Lest I revenge. *What?* my Selfe upon my Selfe?" Here *What* evidently crept in by mistake from the line above.

P. 192. K. Rich.   *O Ratcliff, I fear, I fear!*
    Methought the souls of all that I had murder'd
    Came to my tent; and every one did threat
    To-morrow's vengeance on the head of Richard.
           Rat. Nay, good my lord, be not afraid of shadows. — In the old copies, the last three lines of Richard's speech are placed at the close of Richard's soliloquy, before the entrance of Ratcliff. With this arrangement, there is no apparent ground or reason for Ratcliff's saying, "be not afraid of shadows." The transposition was proposed by Mason.

P. 193. *Methought their souls, whose bodies Richard murder'd,*
    Came to my tent, and cried, On! victory! — So Warburton. The old copies read " and cried *on Victory*." Pope changed this to "cried *out* Victory." Shakespeare has the phrase to *cry on* repeatedly; but in most other cases it means to "exclaim *against*"; a meaning evidently unsuited to the context here.

P. 194. *Sound, drums and trumpets, boldly, cheerfully.* — So Pope and Collier's second folio. The old text has " boldly *and* cheerfully."

P. 195. *They thus directed, we* ourself *will follow,* &c. — So Pope. The old copies lack *ourself*, thus leaving a gap in the verse where, evidently, there ought to be none.

P. 196. *Jockey of Norfolk, be not* too *bold.* — The old copies have " be not *so* bold" and " be not *to* bold." The *Chronicles* suggest the correction.

P. 197. *To desperate* ventures *and assured destruction.* — So Capell. The old copies have *adventures* instead of *ventures*.

P. 197. *They would* distrain *the one, distain the other.* — So Warburton, Walker, and Collier's second folio. The old text has *restraine* instead of *distrain*. The former word was never used in a sense suited to the context, while Shakespeare has the latter twice at least in just the sense here required.   See foot-note 26.

P. 198. *Off with his son George's head !* — Hanmer printed " Off *instantly* with his son George's head," and it would seem that some such qualifying word is fairly required.

ACT V., SCENE 5.

P. 199. They fight, *and exeunt fighting.* — Instead of this, the old copies have " *they fight*, Richard is slaine"; and then add " *Enter Richmond, Derby bearing the Crowne,*" &c.   Here we have a plain contradiction, as Stanley is made to enter, and bring the crown, into the same place where Richard lies dead ; which of course implies the slaying of him to have taken place somewhere else.   But it is ad-mitted, I believe, on all hands, that the stage-directions in the old copies are often badly confused, and that, in many instances at least, they were supplied by the players.   Perhaps it was the custom in Shakespeare's time, as it still is, to have Richard killed before the audience. — I must add, that neither the fourth nor the fifth scene of this Act is so marked in the old copies ; but the course of the action fairly implies a change of scene in both places.   Such changes indeed were often left to the imagination of the audience ; owing, probably, to the scant arrangements for scene-shifting on the old stage.   Here the marking of the fifth scene, though not less necessary than that of the fourth, was left to be made by Dyce.

P. 200. *But tell me* now, *is young George Stanley living ?* — So Dyce.   The old text lacks *now*.   Pope filled up the gap in the metre by inserting *first*.

P. 200. *All this divided York and Lancaster,*
   O, now let Richmond and Elizabeth,
   The true succeeders of each royal House, —
   Divided in their dire division, —
   By God's fair ordinance conjoin together ! — In the old copies, the fourth of these lines is printed as the second.   This arrangement makes the sense very obscure, to say the least, and has caused a deal

of trouble to the editors, who, it seems, cannot yet agree about either the meaning or the punctuation of the passage. Mr. White so punctuates it as to give the same meaning which is here given, except in the first of the five lines, where I think he errs in taking *divided* as a verb, and not as a participle, and so making *York* and *Lancaster* the objects of it ; as if the foregoing particulars were the cause, and not the consequences, of the quarrel. The sense of that line I take to be, " All this *division of* York and Lancaster." And I have little doubt that the fourth line as here printed got transposed, by some mistake, into the place of the second; an error which those who are at all practised in the mysteries of printing can easily understand.

BOOKS IN HIGHER ENGLISH

GINN & COMPANY, Publishers,

Boston.   New York.   Chicago.   Atlanta.   Dallas.